SO-CFR-028

Children's Music Ministry:

A GUIDE TO PHILOSOPHY AND PRACTICE

Children's Music Ministry:

A GUIDE TO PHILOSOPHY AND PRACTICE

Children's Music Ministry:

A GUIDE TO PHILOSOPHY AND PRACTICE

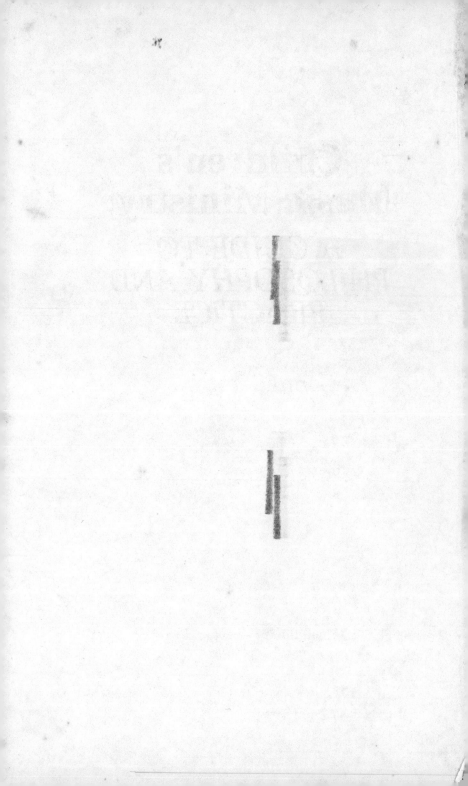

To my husband, Jim,
whose life embodies the essence of music ministry–
musical and spiritual integrity

Contents

Foreword

What most deeply troubles the Christian layman and clergy today is the frightening gulf that has developed between the Church's worship and its ethical witness in the world. Something serious has gone wrong, and one suspects that it has to do not the least with its attitude toward Christian worship.

By definition, worship is the worship of God, not just a pious human experience. We praise God in worship simply because God exists and is God; we delight in Him in His own nature and for His own sake. We adore God in Himself as the End beyond all other ends. Worship thus considered is man's giving himself up in awe to the essence of things, a sharing in the divine plan that sustains and moves the world.

In recent years we have seen the Church scramble to reconceive worship out of anxiety for its impact upon the secular world. However, these changes have merely attempted to keep pace with cultural taste changes and have had little or nothing to do with substance. When observing these attempts, one is reminded of Dean William R. Inge's statement some years ago that when the Church marries the spirit of the age, she will be left a widow in the next generation.

As the smoke has cleared from the late 1960s and 1970s, we have discovered that what the Church really owes the world is not her cleverness and adaptability but simply obedience to the Gospel. In our desire for church growth, we have failed to educate the congregation—young and old alike—in some of the fundamental principles of Christian worship. If we are to stem the tide, we must develop a systematic program of Christian education—in both the church and the private Christian school—that will instill these concepts at an early age.

One place to begin is with a children's music ministry.

Church musicians sometimes forget that the most important choir is the congregation. It is here, within the context of corporate worship, that a right relationship between the liturgical and aesthetic life of the church commences. What a wonderful and exciting prospect for the musician who is committed to a life of musical service in Christian education. Through a well-planned and effectively executed children's music ministry, the fundamental principles of biblical Christianity can be taught, and the nature of worship as a personal response to the Word of God can be reinforced.

The key to all this is a clear understanding of the New Testament term *worship* as meaning not only that which happens on Sunday morning at a certain time and place but what takes place in the believer's total existence. In short, the thrust of our understanding of a biblical, and especially a New Testament, concept of worship moves us to view the Christian life in its totality as a *liturgical* life. As used in this context, the term *liturgy* refers to the "service" or "work" of "the people" and is variously applied in Scripture to the service of Zechariah in the Temple (Lk. 1:23), the worship of Christ (Heb. 8:6) and of the church (Acts 13:2), to the collection of money for the apostolic missions (II Cor. 9:12), to the labors of Epaphroditus (Phil. 2:30), to the prayer of the people, and even to the impending death of St. Paul (Phil. 2:17).

The importance of individual participation in the "body life" of the congregation cannot be overemphasized. In the New Testament, and especially in the letters of Paul, there is an ongoing concern for "building" or edifying." In the words of Karl Barth, "If it [worship] does not take place here, it does not take place anywhere." Therefore, if we are to discover the true model for the individual believer's role in the Church's liturgical life, we may look to God's people at Corinth, each of whom contributed "a hymn, some instruction, a revelation, an ecstatic utterance, or the interpretation of such an utterance" all aimed "at one thing: to build up the church" (I Cor. 14:26, NEB).

Music can and does serve as a powerful force in this process. In this book, Connie Fortunato has made a remarkable contribution by placing the musical training of the child clearly and logically at the center of the Christian education program. As she states so decisively, "Music *does* belong at the core of the curriculum," and "Music *is* essential in the child's development of a world view—in relationship to himself, his God, and his world" (emphasis mine). A children's music ministry designed around these principles will make a significant difference in the life of the Church.

RAY ROBINSON

Princeton, New Jersey
January 2, 1981

Introduction

THIS IS A BOOK about children and music. But it doesn't start with stick-on beards, terry-cloth robes, or any of the other standard church program paraphernalia. It doesn't even start with learning to sit still and keep eyes on the director.

No, it starts further back.

Children's music can make a significant contribution to the spiritual life of the church, but only if it is allowed to be more than "little dears doing ditties." Before we can work children's music into a vital part of the church's ministry, we must first understand the larger role of music itself in the life of God's people. Only then can we apply the child-factor to the overall music ministry.

Thus, chapters 1-4 of this book will take the broad view—seeing how music fits into God's plan for the church. Then, the second and third parts of the book will narrow the focus to an often overlooked but tremendously important ministry—children's music.

The field of children's music has undergone extensive change in the last twenty-five years. Music instruction usually was not begun until the middle childhood years, somewhere around the age of 8, and then it progressed in rather disciplined academic fashion until it was determined whether or not a child was "musically inclined."

Those who received a "musically inclined" rating were given continued musical opportunities. Those not judged to be "musical" generally were steered away from musical involvements by parents and music teachers with a condescending "Honey, you can't carry a tune in a bucket—maybe you should play baseball or learn to sew." Children's choirs in the church were rare. They usually could be found only in larger, rather affluent churches where the emphasis on regular musical performance demanded a rather elitist group of musically advanced children. Music education, if it existed at all, was viewed as secondary to performance, which provided some beneficial activities, but limited music education to an "only as we have time" basis.

This characterization is rapidly becoming antiquated. In the secular world, music education for very young children—some beginning as early as three years old—has mushroomed into an area of its own specialization. With the development of music educators such as Zoltan Kodaly, Carl Orff, Madeline Carabo-Cone, Suzuki, and Robert Pace, and the research of organizations such as the Yamaha Learning Explorations, research, theory, and practice have all proven that early childhood is the prime time for music instruction. Entire schools of music instruction for very young children, based on the philosophy and practice of these people, are in operation around the world.

These philosophies and developments are not limited to instruction of the very young. Their implications have revised the entire approach and methodology of music pedagogy. The theory, being confirmed by these schools, suggests, that because music is experienced through the ear, and primary ear development takes place in early childhood, music can, and should be, learned in a sequence of "experience first—then learn" rather than the previous approach of "analyze academically first—then experience." The phrase "musically inclined," educators are realizing, is more a reflection of the musical environment and exposure provided for a child than the evaluation of some musical "gift" that some children possess and others do not. Music is coming to be seen as a characteristic of all children.

The church is beginning to reflect these changes in attitude and practice in music education. Children's choirs are increasing in number annually. No longer are they limited to exceptionally large churches, but now are integral programs in many churches of average size. Many denominations as well as interdenominational organizations now sponsor children's music festivals, music camps, and training seminars for children's music directors. Many churches are instituting schools of fine arts and comprehensive music education programs for their children. The trend is intensifying.

There is little doubt that the next decade will place the church music minister at the core of music education in the community.

The challenge and opportunities are exciting! Along with the opportunity come the risks—the hazards—and the ensuing needs. There is the hazard of not being equipped to meet the demand—and the need for curriculum materials and trained leadership. There is the hazard of building a program based on individual whims and personal preferences—and the need for a clear purpose based on a biblical foundation. There is the hazard of operating without clear direction so that no real progress or effectiveness is actualized—and the need for a clear statement of specific objectives and a yardstick for measuring actual progress.

Music in the church has generated extensive dialogue, and in many instances, heated debate, throughout church history. Luther's Reformation involved not only doctrinal dispute but also allowed the congregation to take part in hymn singing, rather than limiting musical participation to the priesthood. The middle of the sixteenth century saw the Council of Trent engaged in heated debate over the use of polyphony and elaborate musical settings instead of the traditional plainsong and Gregorian chant. Today, music committees and ministers of music spend countless hours planning the music for their local churches, trying to select music that will satisfy everyone's personal taste.

Many churches operate without a clear statement of philosophy of music. Churches that do have a stated philosophy of music are frequently the victims of some person who has gerrymandered the philosophy to align with personal preference or reaction. This unbalanced approach not only creates ill will in the adult membership of the church, but the children bear the brunt of this fragmentation. A children's music program that is born in this environment will inherit the deformities and weaknesses of the parent program.

Scripture is filled with musical references and illustrations as well as injunctions and commandments for proper use. Scripture contains a comprehensive philosophy of music for the corporate church body and ample teaching on the role of music in the life of the believer. A music program that is based on biblical premises will generate health in the life of the church—both corporately and individually. A clear understanding of biblical models will determine our "modus operandi" on all levels of ministry—adult and children.

What is needed, then, is an examination of biblical principles and a tool for implementing them in our generation. Children's music ministry need not be a passing fancy. Understanding our purpose, from a biblical perspective, and our practice, from the perspective of current research and developments, will bring our children's music programs into maturity for Christ and his Kingdom. This book is an attempt to provide both purpose and practice for all who administrate and direct children's music programs.

Part One

BIBLICAL
PERSPECTIVES

1
Musical Function in the Bible

Sing for joy to God our strength;
Shout joyfully to the God of Jacob.
Raise a song, strike the timbrel,
The sweet sounding lyre with the harp.
Blow the trumpet at the new moon,
At the full moon, on our feast day.
For it is a statute for Israel,
An ordinance of the God of Jacob.
Psalm 81:1-4

MUSIC IS COMMANDED in Scripture! Even the casual Bible student cannot neglect the repeated injunctions to "sing unto the Lord," "declare his majesty," or to "teach and admonish one another," and all are to take the form of musical expression.

The subject of music occupies a prominent place in Scripture. The innumerable times we are commanded to "sing to the Lord" or "come into his presence with singing" make it apparent that God must enjoy music. While it may be impossible to analyze the nature of his enjoyment, it is our responsibility to return to him this gift of music as he commanded. Music is an expression *to* God!

Let the word of Christ richly dwell within you, with all wisdom teaching and admonishing one another with psalms and hymns and spiritual songs, singing with thankfulness in your hearts to God.
Colossians 3:16

3

Scripture also clearly teaches that music is an expression to other members within the Body of Christ. "Let the word of Christ dwell richly within you, with all wisdom . . ." may be taken as a biblical definition of Christian education. Scripture never defines Christian maturity or Christian education in terms of accumulation of assorted biblical facts or phenomena, but rather in terms of *internalization* and *application* of fundamental truth. Music is an essential ingredient in this process.

> Sing to the Lord a new song;
> Sing to the Lord, all the earth.
> Sing to the Lord, bless His name;
> Proclaim good tidings of His salvation
>   from day to day.
> Tell of His glory among the nations,
> His wonderful deeds among all the peoples.
> For great is the Lord, and greatly to be praised;
> He is to be feared above all gods.
> Psalm 96:1-4

Finally, Scripture clearly illustrates that music is an expression to those who have "other gods," those who are outside the spiritual body of the church. Music is a means of proclaiming his salvation, telling his glory, and declaring his wonderful deeds. The relationship between music and sharing the good news is as old as the Old Testament itself.

Music is a God-given gift. Not only did God create music for his own pleasure, but for the fulfillment of human beings—fulfillment on every level—intellectually, emotionally, physically, and spiritually. To reduce music to filler, designed either as preliminaries in our adult services, or as a tool to burn off steam or take up time because we ran out of things to do in our children's ministries, is to prostitute and degrade this God-given expression.

Even if people understand the biblical significance of music, they may try to rank it in some sort of structured hierarchy or priorital preference. Not only is such prioritizing dangerous because it cannot be substantiated in Scripture, but it places fulfillment of all the purposes of music at the mercy of human allocation. To regard music that is an expression to God as more spiritual than that which "de-

4

clares his glory among the heathen" is clearly a violation of biblical principle. It is interesting to note in the three passages cited earlier in this chapter (Ps. 81:1-4; Col. 3:16; Ps. 96:1-4) that although the *function* of music is different, the *purpose* is the same. Each description is clearly portrayed with the overriding purpose of being "to God." Even Colossians 3:16 finishes with this perspective, that it is "to God." It is imperative, then, that we understand that whether the function of music is worship, education (edification), or evangelism, it is never different in purpose or the ultimate Person to whom it is directed. It cannot be ranked by priority or personal preference. It is all to the glory of God.

MUSIC AS WORSHIP

O come, let us sing for joy to the Lord;
Let us shout joyfully to the rock of our salvation.
Let us come before His presence with thanksgiving;
Let us shout joyfully to Him with psalms.
For the Lord is a great God. . . .
Come, let us worship and bow down.
Psalm 95:1-6

God created us for spiritual fellowship. The ability to communicate with God distinguishes us from all other creation. When God designed creation, mankind was the only creature fashioned in the image of God. It is this spiritual fellowship—the coming to God, focusing our complete attention on him, and responding to his character—that defines worship.

Worship is an offering to God. God is the audience, the recipient. Genesis 22:5 states, "And Abraham said to his young men, 'Stay here with the donkey, and I and the lad will go yonder; *and we will worship* and return to you.'" The setting is well known. God had told Abraham to present his son Isaac as a sacrifice *to him*. Abraham prepared to obey God, and just as he was about to slay his own son, God provided a ram caught in a thicket for the burnt offering. And yet, even before Abraham knew the final outcome, he defined his sacrifice to God as worship.

Worship is required by God. In Deuteronomy 26, God is

5

giving the laws to the Israelites requiring the firstfruits of their produce.

> Then it shall be, when you enter the land which the Lord your God gives you as an inheritance, and you possess it and live in it, that you shall take some of the first of all the produce of the ground which you shall bring in from your land that the Lord your God gives you, and you shall put it in a basket . . . And you shall set it down before the Lord your God, and worship before the Lord your God.
> *Deuteronomy 26:1-2; 10*

God's demand for worship is exclusive. "For you shall not worship any other god, for the Lord whose name is Jealous, is a jealous God" (Ex. 34:14). God's warning is even stronger in Deuteronomy 30:17-18: "But if your heart turns away and you will not obey, but are drawn away and worship other gods and serve them, I declare to you today that you shall surely perish."

Worship recognizes God's character. Psalm 96, which is a song calling the people to worship, states:

> Ascribe to the Lord, O families of the peoples,
> Ascribe to the Lord glory and strength.
> Ascribe to the Lord the glory of His name;
> Bring an offering, and come into His courts.
> Worship the Lord in holy attire;
> Tremble before Him, all the earth.
> *Psalm 96:7-9*

Worship places God and humans in their proper relationship. "We are His people and the sheep of His pasture" (Ps. 100:3). A true understanding of who God is, and who we are, places us in a position of obeisance and humility. Frequent Old Testament references call for falling down on one's face, "worshiping at his footstool," or "bowing down." Psalm 95:6 instructs, "Come, let us worship and bow down. Let us kneel before the Lord our Maker." Psalm 99:5 states, "Exalt the Lord our God, And worship at His footstool; Holy is He."

Worship requires intellect and emotion. In the New Testament, the Lord Jesus teaches concerning worship.

> But an hour is coming, and now is, when the true worshipers
> shall worship the Father in spirit and truth; for such people the
> Father seeks to be His worshipers. God is spirit; and those who
> worship Him must worship in spirit and truth.
> *John 4:23, 24*

Not only do these verses reiterate God's desire for worship,
but they clearly define the essence of worship: "spirit"—the
subjective dimension of the personality, the emotion or feeling part of communication characterized by praise, thankfulness, reverence, dedication, confession, or petition—and
"truth"—the intellectual dimension of the personality, the
knowing of God, the statement of his character, his worthiness, and his holiness.

*Music has been an essential ingredient in worship since
the days of the Old Testament.* The examples of music we
find in the Bible not only fit the biblical definition of
worship, but also demonstrate that combination of spirit and
truth, intellect and emotion, that Christ said was necessary
for genuine worship.

The song of Moses in Exodus 15 was sung *to the Lord* as an
offering of praise and thanksgiving for his deliverance from
Egyptian bondage. It recognizes God's character:

> Who is like Thee among the gods, O Lord?
> Who is like Thee, majestic in holiness.
> Awesome in praises, working wonders?
> Thou didst stretch out Thy right hand,
> The earth swallowed them.
> In Thy lovingkindness Thou hast led the people whom Thou hast
>   redeemed;
> In Thy strength Thou has guided them to Thy Holy habitation.
> *Exodus 15:11-13*

Hannah's song in I Samuel 2 and Mary's "Magnificat" in
Luke 1:46-55 are both songs of worship. Each shows an
understanding of the nature of worship. This is true worship
music. It is an expression to God; it recognizes God's character; it places God and man in proper perspective. Mary
says it so precisely when she sings, "My spirit has rejoiced
in God my Savior." Each song is filled with intellectual and
emotional content—they are both "spirit" and "truth."

Worship music may express thanksgiving.

O give thanks to the Lord, for He is good;
For His lovingkindness is everlasting.
Psalm 107:1

Worship music may express dedication and commitment.

I love Thee, O Lord, my strength.
The Lord is my rock and my fortress and my deliverer,
My God, my rock, in whom I take refuge;
My shield and the horn of my salvation, my stronghold.
Psalm 18:1-2

Worship music may express confession.

Be gracious to me, O God, according to Thy lovingkindness;
According to the greatness of Thy compassion blot out my transgressions.
Wash me thoroughly from my iniquity,
And cleanse me from my sin.
Psalm 51:1-2

Worship music may also take the form of petition.

Give ear to my prayer, O God;
And do not hide Thyself from my supplication.
Psalm 55:1

Music and worship are inextricably linked in Scripture. Music programs—whether for adults or children—need to recognize this fact in principle and practice. Worship music is a corporate and individual expression, but it is always an expression to God. Churches and children's programs that limit their music to personal expressions of daily experiences deny the biblical injunction to "sing to the Lord." We must never confuse our audience. Music that is directed to people—whether to build them up in the faith or relate the claims of Christ—may be valid musical expressions, but they were never intended to be worship or replace the music that is sung to God.

Worship music is commanded in Scripture. It is not a matter of personal preference or congregational identity. It is not limited to a specific age group nor defined by a certain liturgy. To deny individual and corporate worship music is to violate the biblical mandate.

Children are capable of true worship. They need to participate in songs of praise and thanksgiving to God, songs that give glory to God, songs that convey personal commitment and dedication, and songs that express their prayers. Unfortunately, many of our children are deprived from experiencing biblical worship because their music does not embody any of these characteristics. To deny a child the opportunity for true worship only postpones his discovery of why God made him—for spiritual fellowship—and prevents his development of this essential communication during the most formative and impressionable years of life.

The first question, then, in evaluating a children's music program is "Does it include music that is worship?" Are we fulfilling the first musical commandment to "sing to the Lord"?

MUSIC AS EDUCATION

Let the word of Christ richly dwell within you, with all wisdom teaching and admonishing one another with psalms and hymns and spiritual songs, singing with thankfulness in your hearts to God.
Colossians 3:16

Not only does Scripture command music that is worship to God, but it also commands music that is instruction or education for God's people. The relationship between biblical teaching and music is also clearly established in Scripture.

Music is significant in the instruction of the believer. Educational music is addressed not to God but to the child of the God—the believer, the Body of Christ. Colossians 3:16 makes this clear—"teaching and admonishing *one another*." Ephesians 5:19 also emphasizes this focus—"speaking to one another in psalms. . . ." Thus it is clear that music that focuses on biblical instruction is directed to the people of God. Also, if it is to be profitable or valuable, its content should be characterized by teaching, reproof (doctrine), correction, and instruction in righteousness.

9

Music is significant in the instruction of doctrine. One of the most poignant examples of a song that teaches the nature of God as caretaker and provider for his children is the best-loved song throughout history—the Twenty-third Psalm. In verse 1 we find him as the shepherd—the caretaker. In verse 2, the guide; in verse 3, the restorer; in verse 4, the comforter; in verse 5, the provider; and in verse 6, the giver of goodness, kindness, and finally an eternal reward.

Psalm 91 is another song of biblical instruction, teaching that God is the protector of his people.

> He who dwells in the shelter of the Most High
> Will abide in the shadow of the Almighty.
> I will say to the Lord, "My refuge and my fortress,
> My God, in whom I trust!"
> For it is He who delivers you from the snare of the trapper,
> And from the deadly pestilence.
> He will cover you with His pinions,
> And under His wings you may seek refuge;
> His faithfulness is a shield and bulwark.
> *Psalm 91:1-4*

Music is significant in reproof and correction. Reproof and correction are two sides of the same coin. In the educational process, it is the teacher who reproves, pointing out error, and it is the student who then corrects, making the necessary adjustments to make right what was wrong. Music has a unique ability to serve as a mirror, letting us clearly see our mistakes. Many times the words of a song will reprove us, show us our mistake, so that we can correct our wrong.

Psalm 37 provides a beautiful illustration of a song of reproof. It points out clearly the mistake of evaluating prosperity in terms of temporal affluence:

> Rest in the Lord and wait patiently for Him;
> Fret not yourself because of him who prospers in his way,
> Because of the man who carries out wicked schemes.
> Cease from anger, and forsake wrath;
> Fret not yourself, it leads only to evildoing.
> For evildoers will be cut off,
> But those who wait for the Lord, they will inherit the land.
> Yet a little while and the wicked man will be no more;

And you will look carefully for his place, and he will not be
there.
But the humble will inherit the land,
And will delight themselves in abundant prosperity.
Psalm 37:7-11

Music is significant in instruction in righteousness.
Many things are taught more easily and more effectively
through music. Many times we remember the words of a
song when we forget the main points of a sermon. God undoubtedly knew this when he commanded music as part of
"teaching and admonishing one another."

It is interesting to note that Moses, after he had finished
his lengthy instruction to all of Israel, used a song to help the
people remember everything he had said. To insure their
remembrance, he did two things. First, he wrote down the
entire Law and made it into a book and instructed the Levites who carried the Ark of the Covenant to place the book
right beside the Ark so it would always be available as a
written record (Deut. 31:26). But then, "Moses spoke in the
hearing of all the assembly of Israel the words of this song
until they were complete" (Deut. 31:30). The next forty-three
verses contain Moses' instruction for the people—a song. It
is safe to assume that Moses didn't expect the people to
memorize everything he had told them—there were too
many laws, which is why he wrote them down. Then they
could constantly refer to it. But he did want them to remember the essence of God's law—and to have it internalized in
their minds and hearts—so he sang it to them.

Our second consideration, then, in developing a biblical
philosophy of music is to link our music with the educational process of the believer. Much doctrine, reproof, correction, and instruction in righteousness can be achieved effectively through music. While it is not uncommon for much
adult music to have doctrinal content, it is a frequently omitted ingredient in much of our children's repertoire. Faithful-
ness to the Bible demands that we evaluate our music in
terms of significant instructional content. We never outgrow
our need for learning, but to delay the educational process
until adult life is to insure failure. Scripture places much
emphasis on childhood education.

11

Proverbs 22:6 tells us, "Train up a child in the way he should go, Even when he is old he will not depart from it." Many parents and church workers who wonder why they have such a problem with older persons going astray would do well to reevaluate their children's programs and training time in the light of significant content. The problem comes when so much time is spent in "religious activities" rather than in learning the Scripture and God's Law.

Paul reinforces the fact that childhood is the best time to learn Scripture—"From childhood you have known the sacred writings which are able to give you the wisdom that leads to salvation through faith which is in Christ Jesus" (II Tim. 3:15).

To deprive our children of music that will help them in Scripture memorization, aid them in internalizing doctrine, and provide for them reproof and correction is to ignore a biblical principle. We have no right to expect that our children will be "adequately equipped for every good work," and "not departing from the way" if we do not meet the prerequisite. Music can help us achieve our goal.

MUSIC AS EVANGELISM

Hear this, all peoples;
Give ear, all inhabitants of the world.
Both low and high,
Rich and poor together.
My mouth will speak wisdom;
And the meditation of my heart will be understanding.
Psalm 49:1-3

This psalm is credited to the sons of Korah. It is obvious from the opening statement that the song is directed to "all peoples." The singer goes on to ask why one should fear the wealthy and the powerful when wise men and stupid men alike perish and leave their wealth to others. The answer to his riddle is found in verse 15, which says, "But God will redeem my soul from the power of Sheol; For He will receive me." The purpose of the song is to proclaim the answer to the riddle: God's redemption.

Evangelism is the proclamation to everyone of God's provision. Although characteristically seen in a New Testament perspective, evangelism was an Old Testament practice. Although much of the Old Testament emphasized God's dealings with his chosen people, the nation of Israel, "declaring his glory among the heathen" was still a part of Israel's responsibility. Israel was not alone in the task of spreading the message to the ends of the earth. Many of the wonderful acts of God were done as a testimony to his character.

> The heavens are telling of the glory of God;
> And the firmament is declaring the work of His hands.
> Day to day pours forth speech,
> And night to night reveals knowledge.
> There is no speech, nor are there words;
> Their voice is not heard.
> Their line has gone out through all the earth,
> And their utterances to the end of the world.
> *Psalm 19:1-4*

There were even times when Israel petitioned God's favor on the grounds that it would be a testimony to him.

> God be gracious to us and bless us,
> And cause His face to shine upon us—
> That Thy way may be known on the earth,
> Thy salvation among all nations.
> *Psalm 67:1-2*

Isaiah has been called the "evangelical" prophet. Many of the orations recorded in Isaiah—which well may have taken song form—were directed to the nations of Babylon, Tyre, Damascus, and Moab. Jonah was sent to the Assyrian city of Nineveh to cry against its wickedness and cause the people to repent.

Christ commanded evangelism in the New Testament when he told his disciples, "Go into all the world and preach the gospel to all creation" (Mk. 16:15). Evangelism is both a *corporate* and an *individual* responsibility.

The New Testament does not give us illustrations of evangelism music; however we must remember that the New Testament church used the music from the Old Testament in their worship, education, and evangelism. It is interesting to note that when Paul and Silas were incarcerated in the Philippian prison, they didn't spend their time trying to argue their theology or preach a sermon—which they were well qualified to do. Instead, "about midnight Paul and Silas were praying and singing hymns of praise to God, and the prisoners were listening to them" (Acts 16:25). The earthquake followed, and the jailer was about to commit suicide when Paul and Silas reassured him that no one had even tried to escape; they all were present. We don't know how many of the other prisoners accepted Christ along with the jailer and his family that night. But we do know that they heard about God through the singing of Paul and Silas.

It is in keeping with biblical illustrations to assume that evangelistic music may be expressed in different ways. It may be an outright declaration of the glory of God or the person of his Son; it may be in the form of a riddle, articulating a contemporary question and providing a biblical solution; it may be a personal expression of what God has done in the individual's life; or it may point out the many great wonders of God's hand—but all with the same result: the declaration of God among all peoples.

Children are marvelous communicators. They are able to speak in places and in ways that adults cannot. Too many times the opportunity to participate in evangelism has been reserved for the adult—the theologian, the intellectual, the philosopher. And yet Christ made it incredibly clear to the adults that "unless you are converted and become like children, you shall not enter the kingdom of heaven. Whoever then humbles himself as this child, he is the greatest in the kingdom of heaven" (Mt. 18:3, 4).

When evangelism is cultivated as a natural part of self-expression and communication during childhood, it perpetuates practicing evangelism in adulthood. Many adults are terrorized at the commandment to "make His glory known among the heathen" because they "don't know how" or have never done it, or don't know what to say. Music provides a natural means of communication, and yet adults who did not participate in musical expressions as children frequently find the idea of singing their message as terrifying as giving a public testimony.

Many times a song can reach where the spoken word cannot. Because music has the ability to speak differently to the feelings and emotions of a person, it frequently finds entrance where all else finds barriers. In I Samuel 16:14-23, we read the account of Saul tormented by the evil spirit. His servants recommended that Saul seek out a skillful musician to come and play the harp, that he might be refreshed and be made well.

Many times music will be requested, and these can be turned into an opportunity for evangelism. Children who are given songs declaring God's character, his redemption, and its personal application in their own lives will have opportunity to share this message in school, with friends, with relatives, and many times even in their own homes to unbelieving family members.

Music is an effective tool in evangelism. We must recognize this important relationship in the music we select for our children as well as our congregations at large. Children who have participated in evangelism music in the church will be better able to share their faith in the world. The opportunity is available. Many places extend warm invitations for children's choirs. To gain these opportunities, however, our preparation must be responsible. Music is significant in evangelism. It belongs in the hands of our children.

CONCLUSION

Music is commanded in Scripture. Along with this commandment comes an abundance of instruction regarding the philosophy and practice of music. Being faithful to biblical principles is paramount for a truly Christian music ministry—whether adult- or child-oriented. Children's music ministry is not exempt from biblical principles.

A music ministry that rests on a biblical foundation will have three prevailing audiences and three resulting ministries. First, we must offer music that is worship. Scripture teaches that worship is an offering to God, worship is required by God, God's demand for worship is exclusive, worship recognizes God's character, worship places God and humans in their proper perspective, and true worship requires both intellect and emotion. Music was established as an essential ingredient in worship in the Old Testament. A diagram of the participant and the audience could be drawn like this:

God (the audience)

↑

The singer (participating in worship)

Worship does not depend on surroundings or liturgies. Worship is not an expression to us; it is addressed to God. Our first criterion for evaluation of our music, then, is to examine our repertoire to see if we are obeying the command to "sing to the Lord."

Second, *we must offer music that is an expression to the Body of Christ.* Our role in the Body of Christ is to teach and admonish, to encourage and build up in the faith, that we may be fully equipped to do all good works. We are commanded to grow into the full stature of Christ Jesus. Growth comes through knowledge of the Word of God. Music was instrumental in teaching the Law in the Old Testament and was commanded as a method of Bible instruction in the New Testament. Knowledge of Scripture provides doctrine, reproof, correction, and instruction in righteousness for the child of God. Scripture places much emphasis on the importance of childhood education. If music is to fulfill its God-given responsibility, it must be substantially linked to the education of the believer. Although the message is directed to the Body of Christ, it is ultimately for God's glory since the maturation of His people is a source of glory to Him. Education music could be diagrammed as follows:

God (receiving the ultimate glory)

↖

The children of God (either mutually participating
or listening)

↗

The singer (participating in teaching and admonishing)

Finally, *we must provide music that is designed to declare salvation to the unbeliever.* Again, Scripture provides us with a clear definition of evangelism and examples of music sung corporately and individually as testimony of the Lord

16

God. The fact that music provides a powerful medium for communication is established in Scripture and is still observable today. The Lord placed a child in the middle of the adults when he wanted to teach about coming into his Kingdom. Children are powerful communicators and deserve our attention when it comes to presenting the claims of the gospel. The redemption of mankind was God's purpose in providing a Savior. Redemption points to God. Music that is significant in evangelism could be diagramed this way:

God (ultimately glorified in the redemption of man)
↑
The hearer (a person outside the family of God)
↑
The singer (expressing the nature of God, his mighty
                acts, or relating a personal experience, etc.)

We must provide a balance in our musical emphasis, just as the Bible does. To emphasize one area at the expense of another, regardless of reason, is to deny God's intention. Scripture does not make worship music more "spiritual" than evangelism music. Both are commanded. Both are necessary to fulfill God's law. Nor does Scripture endorse the practice of evangelization or edification without time set aside for worship. This biblical understanding of philosophy and function must permeate every department if our music ministry is to be acceptable in the sight of God.

2
Musical Types in the Bible

Speaking to one another in psalms and hymns and spiritual songs, singing and making melody with your heart to the Lord.
Ephesians 5:19

WHILE THE PRESENCE OF MUSIC in the church throughout history may be a common characteristic of Judeo-Christian tradition, the type of music performed has created heated debate and bitter arguments for hundreds of years. The (Council of Trent (held intermittently between 1545 and 1563) found itself in heated debate over the use of polyphony—a complex musical style of usually four parts, all operating independently, rather than in strict parallel motion (organum). It was contended that the use of polyphony was too secular for the church because much of the textual content was lost in the ornate musical setting.

Today is not much different. Some speakers angrily denounce the "evils" of contemporary religious music, while others resist much of the traditional church music because the antiquated language and archaic musical settings make it "irrelevant" and "out of touch" with their people. Music committees and music ministers spend countless hours trying to decide on music compatible with the personality of their congregation.

Because music involves personal participation and embodies personal expression, and since people feel they have a right to determine what they will or will not participate in, music becomes the one area of church life where everyone feels entitled to an opinion. Musically trained leadership frequently tries to deny this "right to opinion" by the non-musician, and scores of musically untrained congregations consider the musician's tastes limited and unable to relate to the music they like.

In the heat of personal preference we have frequently forgotten that Scripture gives some clear guidelines regarding type of music. Are choruses a valid musical expression? What role do hymns play in the life of the church? Are they important, or should they be artistically buried in the ornate vaults of history? What about contemporary music? Does music need to be around for fifty years before it becomes "of age"?

While it is true that the lines defining musical genre are subtle and frequently overlap, it is also true that different types of music outlined in Scripture differ in their characteristics. While it is not our purpose to "nit-pick," we must identify these prominent musical characteristics in order to establish principles of musical selection based on a biblical perspective, rather than clutching to tradition or following every fad. Responsible music selection for children and adults demands a clear understanding of the types of music mentioned in the Bible.

PSALM SINGING

Psalm singing is the oldest known form of vocal music. Psalm singing is the most prevalent musical practice in Scripture. The most noted musician in the Bible, David, was referred to as "the psalmist" (2 Sam. 23:1).

What were the prominent musical features of psalms? How did they function in corporate and individual expression? How have they developed through the years, and what should be noted in establishing guidelines for music selection today?

Textually, psalms were predominantly Scripture singing, although the term was applicable to any elements of the Jewish service that lent themselves to musical renditions. They were characteristically a free-flowing poetic form. Because the nature of the text was free-flowing, the musical setting was also rather free and unregimented. The music was governed by the syntactic accents and could vary in length from phrase to phrase or section to section. The *Encyclopedia Judaica* defines the textual style this way:

> Its outlines and internal organization follow closely those of the poetic form. Each psalm may consist of a smaller or greater number of verses, without being organized in symmetrical stanzas. Accordingly, the melody of one verse may become a musical unit which is repeated as many times as there are verses in the psalm. . . . The biblical verse is formed and characterized solely by the number of its stressed syllables, disregarding completely how many weak syllables there are between the stresses. The verses of a psalm may consequently vary widely in length, since the overall number of syllables is not constant. The tune has to be adaptable to these floating conditions.[1]

Musically, psalm singing was a simple melody—basically centered on one main note—the "recitation note." There were eight different recitation notes to choose from—undoubtedly the forerunners of the eight Greek modes—an important historical link in the development of church music. The recitation tone was always the dominant (or "fifth note") of the mode, and was initiated by a few introductory notes called the "initium." The melodic form was binary, consisting of two sections each initiated by an "initium," followed by the "recitation note," and completed by a cadence. The use of the recitation note guaranteed the flexibility needed by the irregular texts.[2]

Structurally, there were three forms of psalmody. The first was direct psalmody, in which a complete psalm or a number of verses were sung by one person—the cantor—without any textual additions or modifications. It is the oldest form of psalmody, and was necessary as a foundation for other forms of psalmody, since it acquainted the people with the scriptural texts as well as the melody. The second form was responsorial psalmody. It quickly replaced direct psalmody in prominence because it allowed opportunity for congregational response. In this form, a verse was sung by the cantor, and then either repeated or affirmed by the congregation or choir with a phrase such as "Amen" or with a sentence, as we see in Psalm 136:

> Give thanks to the Lord, for He is good;
> For His lovingkindness is everlasting.

Give thanks to the God of gods,
For His lovingkindness is everlasting.
Give thanks to the Lord of lords,
For His lovingkindness is everlasting.
To Him who alone does great wonders,
For His lovingkindness is everlasting.

And so the alternating between the cantor and the congregation goes on throughout the psalm—similar to our responsive readings today.

The third type of psalmody was _antiphonal psalmody_, which consisted of two half-choruses or choirs. Sometimes one choir would sing the psalm verse and the other the response, or sometimes one would sing the first half of the psalm verse, ending with the medial cadence, and the second chorus would respond by singing the second half of the psalm verse and end with the final cadence. An illustration of antiphonal psalmody is found in Nehemiah 12:31-46:

> Then I had the leaders of Judah come up on top of the wall, and I appointed two great choirs, the first proceeding to the right on top of the wall toward the Refuse Gate.... The second choir proceeded to the left.... Then the two choirs took their stand in the house of God. So did I and half of the officials with me.... and on that day they offered great sacrifices and rejoiced because God had given them great joy, even the women and children rejoiced, so that the joy of Jerusalem was heard from afar.... For they performed the worship of their God and the service of purification, together with the singers and the gatekeepers in accordance with the command of David and of his son Solomon. For in the days of David and Asaph, in ancient times, there were leaders of the singers, songs of praise and hymns of thanksgiving to God.

The setting is described in detail. Nehemiah's dedication service for the wall included antiphonal singing. It is also possible that antiphonal psalmody was the kind of singing used in warfare. In II Chronicles 20:20-22, we have the account of the battle of the Israelites under King Jehoshaphat meeting the armies of Moab. God had said that the battle was his and that the people were to praise him. So Jehoshaphat placed "those who sang to the Lord and those who praised Him in holy attire" in front of the army, and they sang, "Give

21

thanks to the Lord, for His lovingkindness is everlasting."
Presumably one choir sang the first phrase, and the second
"half-chorus" sang the second phrase.

Stylistically, psalm singing was accompanied by a
stringed instrument called the "psaltery," a small hand harp.
In fact this small harp was one of the earliest known instruments. The first reference to music in Scripture is found in
Genesis 4:21 where Jubal is credited with being the "father
of all those who play the lyre (another small stringed instrument) and pipe (an early wind instrument)."

Functionally, psalm singing filled a number of purposes.
Antiphonal psalmody, as we have seen, was used in warfare,
in celebration (as in Exodus 15), in procession (it was very
possibly the form used in I Chronicles 16, when David had
the Ark of the Covenant moved), as well as in the Temple
services to call the people to worship. Direct psalmody was
used by a soloist to recite a Scripture lesson or remind the
people of historic events or teach them a new psalm. However, once the psalm became familiar, direct psalmody was
replaced by responsorial psalmody thereby allowing the
congregation to actively participate in worship. Psalm singing was primarily an act of worship. It was directed to God as
praise, thanksgiving, commitment, confession, and petition.
According to Eric Werner, psalm singing was strongly en-
couraged in private devotions as well as public worship.[3]
Secondarily, however, it must be realized that psalm singing
was significant in the education and edification of God's
people. Responsorial psalmody increased the people's
knowledge of Scripture. As they participated in the singing
of the inspired Word of God, they not only committed much
of its content to memory, but built up one another in the
faith. Throughout history those groups of people participating in psalm singing or Scripture singing have effectively
"hid the Word of God" in their hearts. Few people engage in
the academic discipline of extensive Scripture memorization. However, if the Scriptures are sung, the laborious "discipline" is eliminated, and the Scriptures are easily committed to memory.

Werner sums it up this way, "From the historic point of
view, psalmody was the greatest legacy of the Synagogue to
Jewish Christianity, and thence to the Gentile Church."[4]

HYMN SINGING

Although hymn singing may not be quite as old as psalm singing, it has, nevertheless, been a part of biblical worship since the days of the Old Testament. Its form was undoubtedly taken from responsorial psalmody, where the response took the form of a regular refrain, and thereby gave rise to strophic form—a symmetrical arrangement of music consisting of verse-refrain, verse-refrain.

In biblical times—both Old and New Testament—there is undoubtedly a close relationship between psalm singing and hymn singing. Differences were most likely stylistic—psalmody being always accompanied by the psaltery and hymn singing could be either accompained or a cappella, and hymn singing was done by the entire congregation while psalm singing could be solo, choral, or congregational. Textual differences were also characteristic in that psalm singing most frequently employed a scriptural text, and a hymn could be a non-scriptural poetic text set to music.

It is, therefore, safe to assume that because of the repeated use of these more "regular" texts—whether regular by design or by constant repetition—the music became more formalized and less free-flowing.

Music historians have even traced the names of some of the early hymns. For example, the passage of Psalms 113-118 is called the "Hallel." While Old Testament practices indicated that this psalm was sung responsorially,[5] this is generally regarded to be the hymn that Jesus and his disciples sang following the Last Supper before going out to the Mount of Olives (Mt. 26:30).[6] Undoubtedly in the intervening generations, the repeated use of this passage responsorially contributed sufficiently enough to the people's knowledge of its entire text and melody that it became congregational.

As hymn singing developed and the repertoire increased, the predominance of the recitation note diminished because the flexibility was no longer a prevailing need. Stylized texts gave rise to stylized melodies.

After Christ's ascension, the assembling of believers was not limited to synagogues or the Temple, but small groups of Christians would assemble in homes for worship and praise. As Christianity spread throughout the Greek world, its music became influenced by Greek culture.

The oldest known hymn—other than a scriptural text—is attributed to Clement of Alexandria in about A.D. 170.

Shepherd of tender youth,
Guiding in loving truth,
Through devious ways;
Christ, our triumphant King,
We come Thy Name to sing,
Hither the children bring
Tributes of praise.
Translated by Henry Martin Dexter,
Nineteenth century[7]

The earliest Christian hymn for which both text and melody have been preserved is the Oxyrhynchus hymn, dating from A.D. 270, discovered in Middle Egypt. The text of this hymn is Greek, and the melody appeared in Greek vocal notation. A translation of the Greek words legible on the damaged fragment:

... all glorious created things God together ... shall not keep silence nor may the stars beaming light hold back ... all waves of the rushing rivers shall praise our Father, Son and Holy Spirit, all powers join together in: Amen! Amen! Might and praise and glory be to God, He who alone is the Giver of all good things. Amen! Amen![8]

One characteristic noted in each of these examples, which may reveal one of the main reasons for creating hymn texts, is the mention of Christ. Psalms were sung about and to Jehovah God. Not until the coming of Christ and the recognition of his place in the Godhead was there made mention of "Christ, our triumphant King," or "Father, Son, and Holy Spirit" in the texts of worship music. This characteristic even bore mentioning in a letter from Pliny, governor of Bithynia, to the Emperor Trajan, in the year A.D. 112. Pliny wrote that Christians "were in the habit of meeting on a certain fixed day before it was light, when they sang an anthem to Christ as God."[9]

Functionally, hymn singing was closely akin to psalm singing. Hymns were essential in worship—ascribing glory and praise to God and to his Son, Jesus Christ, and in education—transmitting not only the Scriptures, but the doctrinal truths of the church to all participants.

Just as a lack of scriptural knowledge is a commentary on the lack of obedience to the biblical command to "sing psalms," a lack of doctrinal and theological knowledge is a reflection of the neglecting of the biblical injunction to sing hymns.

SPIRITUAL SONGS

Although Paul's injunction in Ephesians and Colossians clearly outlines the use of the spiritual song for the believer, he does not provide us with a clear definition or illustrations. It is, therefore, difficult to establish specific characteristics and criteria. Because of the lack of primary source material, some close their minds as well as their musical exposure to anything other than psalms and hymns. This, however, is obviously a poor choice, since they must ignore this twice-given biblical command as well as historical evidence. Although exact manuscripts have eluded music historians up to this point, we can make some safe assumptions about the predominant characteristics of spiritual songs.

First of all, the spiritual song was a personal expression. It is possible that it began with a soloist or cantor in the synagogue, who at his own liberty inserted an ornate spontaneous expression of joy. It is also more than likely, since Paul obviously had witnessed such expressions, that in the early church spiritual songs had become a way one individual could share spiritual or personal experiences that he felt would benefit the others gathered. Their form of worship was for one to share a portion of Scripture, perhaps one a hymn—in which they could all participate—and another a spiritual song.

This type of expression embodied several musical characteristics. First, the melody and rhythms could be as simple or as complicated as one's ability to perform. Structurally it could be strophic or through-composed—where the singer did not follow a regular verse-chorus pattern, but rather composed new melody throughout to accommodate his text. Textually, it varied considerably from the psalms and hymns because it was a personal expression to the Lord resulting from personal experience. Therefore, its text usually was not taken from Scripture, but focused on topics concerned with daily life.

Functionally, spiritual songs were significant in communicating joy and in establishing identity with an audience. It put the flesh and blood to the truths of Scripture. People in the New Testament no doubt had trouble relating to the experiences of David, just as we today have difficulty identifying with biblical characters. But the person who could relate God's care, God's forgiveness, God's personal love, and the joy of the Lord in day-to-day experiences could bring encouragement to others who were experiencing a difficulty, or provide endorsement to a nonbeliever who needed the personal verification of another.

Because of the validity of this function, spiritual songs began to be handed down from generation to generation. They became so valuable in providing the personal testimony that without them the music of the church would have been limited in content to the expressions of the Israelites and to theological creeds set to music. It is interesting to note that this need for personal testimony was included in Scripture. Many of David's psalms were spontaneous expressions of joy and personal experiences. However, as the centuries passed and David's personality and human qualities became submerged in his historical character, and as his spontaneous expressions became canonized, it became necessary to keep spontaneity alive by creating new spiritual songs.

Although chapter 4 will deal more comprehensively with church music history and its implications for us today, it is interesting to examine the regression of churches who have characteristically denied spiritual songs from their congregations. The split between "form" and "reality," between doctrine and experience, and between recitation and expression has grown from a tiny hairline crack to a wide chasm that places the church, theology, and liturgy on one side and the people on the other.

Churches and generations that have lost the importance of Scripture have lost psalm singing. Churches that have lost doctrine have neglected hymns. But churches that have become mere form and structure have lost their spiritual songs.

CONCLUSION

Principles regarding musical type as a basis for music selection are found in Scripture. Selection of music in our churches—whether for children or adults—is not nearly so much a matter of personal preference as it is a matter of biblical obedience. Three types of music are commanded:

● Psalm singing—singing the Scriptures.

● Hymn singing—the more formalized musical texts, dealing with praise and adoration to God the Father, God the Son, and God the Holy Spirit, and doctrinal and fundamental truth, designed for congregational participation.

● Spiritual songs—the spontaneous, personal, "contemporary" expressions of joy and personal experience.

All three types of music must be used in proper balance if our music programs are to be based on the biblical model.

The problem is not one simply of inclusion versus exclusion. We have a strange tendency to prioritize. Scripture establishes the validity of all types. The sequence of "psalms, hymns, and spiritual songs" is not a priorital arrangement, but rather a sequential arrangement, the order they have generally been used in historical worship. To place a hymn on a higher musical plane than a spiritual song is contrary to the biblical perspective. To negate the personal expression of a believer until it has aged sufficiently to merit a place among the classics is to deny the validity of the spontaneous spiritual song. But to bury the hymns of the past centuries simply because they are not "contemporary" is to reduce our faith and doctrine to the fads of personal fancy.

These principles are not limited to adults. The passage in Nehemiah 12, quoted earlier in this chapter, specifically includes the children. The text of the earliest known hymn refers specifically to children. And if a spiritual song is a personal expression, then the experience of the child is just as valid as that of an adult.

Scriptural parameters are broad. Proper balance is fundamental. To narrow the parameters creates neglect and imbalance in the life of the individual and the corporate Body of Christ. For those wanting to provide music for their children (or adults) that is faithful to the biblical model, all three types of music must be included—psalms, hymns, and spiritual songs.

1. *Encyclopedia Judaica.* (Jerusalem: The Macmillan Co.. Keter Publishing House Ltd., 1971), Vol. 12, p. 572.

2. *Ibid.*

3. Eric Werner, *The Sacred Bridge.* (New York: Columbia University Press, 1959), p. 144.

4. *Ibid.*, p. 145.

5. *Encyclopedia Judaica.* loc. cit., p. 576.

6. John F. Wilson, *An Introduction to Church Music.* (Chicago: Moody Press, 1965), p. 26.

7. *Ibid.*, p. 106.

8. David P. Appleby, *History of Church Music.* (Chicago: Moody Press, 1965), p. 26.

9. Pliny, *Letters*, x.96.

3
Musical Structure in the Bible

Then David spoke to the chiefs of the Levites to appoint their relatives the singers, with instruments of music, harps, lyres, loud-sounding cymbals, to raise sounds of joy.
I Chronicles 15:16

WE HAVE LOOKED at the biblical model for the *function* and the *type* of music ministry in the church. Now we will investigate the *structure* suggested in the Bible.

No period in church music history can compare, either in terms of choirs, instrumentalists, or professional leadership, with the musical productions in the Old Testament during the reigns of David and Solomon. "A great choir of some four thousand musicians and vocalists was gathered and trained; great religious musical festivals were organized, and systematic praise became a permanent feature of Hebrew worship."[1] Our most extravagant pageantry today, complete with orchestra, costumes, and multiple choirs cannot begin to compare with the comprehensive music programs of the nation of Israel.

This musical talent did not just happen all of a sudden. It was the result of careful planning and foundation building. David could not have appointed the thousands of singers if he had not had a reservoir of many more singers whose musical training had been an integral part of the educational process throughout the history of the Israelite nation.

Thus it is important, regardless at which end of the spectrum we find ourselves—a small church with the pastor and a few volunteers providing leadership, or a large multiple staff situation—that we take a closer look at Scripture to examine its perspective on the proper structure of a biblical music ministry.

MUSIC AND LEADERSHIP

Music was undoubtedly included in the training of the religious leadership of the Old Testament. Moses, one of the first great leaders of the nation of Israel, was brought up and schooled in the royal Egyptian court of Pharaoh. By the time he made the decision to forsake his Egyptian heritage and lead God's chosen people, he had fully mastered every aspect of Egyptian knowledge, and music instruction almost certainly was one of the daily essentials. His thorough training in music has distinguished him as one of the earliest composers of choral literature of all time, as he led the Israelites in a song of praise after they had crossed the Red Sea in escape from their Egyptian captors:

> I will sing to the Lord, for He is highly exalted;
> The horse and its rider He has hurled into the sea.
> The Lord is my strength and song,
> And He has become my salvation;
> This is my God, and I will praise Him;
> My father's God, and I will extol Him.
> The Lord is a warrior;
> The Lord is His name.
> *Exodus 15:1-3*

Rev. David Breed of Western Theological Seminary states regarding this magnificent song:

> It is evident that this is not the work of a novice; neither is it the expression of those to whom sacred song is an unpracticed art; for, making all proper allowance for the influence of inspiration, its human elements are indicative of thorough culture in this particular department of literature.
>
> It was probably sung antiphonally; Moses and the men upon the one side, answered by Miriam and the women on the other side. It is thus the oldest specimen of choral song in all literature, and it is one of the finest. Scholars have united to give it most unqualified praise.[2]

Moses' song of instruction preceding his death, previously mentioned in chapter 1, is another example of the high degree of poetic and musical proficiency of this great leader of Israel.

Deborah was another leader of Israel who knew music. Her songs of freedom served as an impetus to awaken the people to their unnecessary bondage to Jabin, the king of Hazor. They finally decided to overthrow their oppressors. After their victory, Deborah and Barak led the Israelites in a song of victory, recorded in Judges 5.

Samuel instituted musical training as part of the required "curriculum" for the "sons of the prophets" (I Sam. 10:5). Although their training was not limited to a specific locale, all the prophets were expected to train young men—through an apprenticeship-type relationship—in all the aspects of ministry of the prophet of God. Music was an important part of their tutelage. This educational system was the forerunner of our modern schools of theology and seminaries. It is important to understand that music was included in their training not only because of its value as an academic discipline, but because it was an integral part of worship.

Ezra, Nehemiah, David, and Isaiah provide further illustration of music leadership being characteristic of Israel's religious leadership. But our investigation of music leadership cannot stop with surveying the musical expertise of only these national leaders. David was, perhaps, the most skilled musician in biblical history. Yet, because of the many demands of his position, he found it necessary to appoint specialized music leaders within the house of the Lord. His prolific compositions, his proficiency on the harp, his ability as a soloist, did not give him a "do it all myself" attitude but helped him realize the importance of appointing specialized musicians, that the ministry of music might be fully developed by individuals who could give it priority and full concentration. David realized that more important than his own musical ability was an understanding of the role that music needed to play in the corporate life of the people of God, and that development on every level required delegated leadership who could carry out their ministry in alignment with this comprehensive understanding.

It is important to note that the musicians were chosen from the Levites. The tribe of Levi was the priestly tribe. It

31

was the tribe set apart by God to be the spiritual leaders of the entire nation. Chenaniah, chief of the Levites, was the leader of song (I Chr. 15:22).

Under Chenaniah's leadership were Heman, the grandson of Samuel, Asaph, and Ethan. They were appointed to instrumental leadership, particularly with the cymbals of brass (I Chr. 15:19). Other divisions of instrumentalists were formed for ministry on the psalteries, and another division for performance on the harps. Asaph was named as the chief of the instrumentalists.

Solomon was obviously schooled in music from his father. He perpetuated the prominence of music in the Temple because of his understanding of its proper usage. At the dedication of Solomon's Temple, we have one of the most moving accounts of music in all Scripture:

> And when the priests came forth from the holy place . . . and all the Levitical singers, Asaph, Heman, Jeduthun, and their sons and kinsmen, clothed in fine linen, with cymbals, harps, and lyres, standing east of the altar, and with them one hundred and twenty priests blowing trumpets, in unison when the trumpeters and the singers were to make themselves heard with one voice to praise and to glorify the Lord, and when they lifted up their voice accompanied by trumpets and cymbals and instruments of music, and when they praised the Lord saying, "He indeed is good for His lovingkindness is everlasting," then the house, the house of the Lord, was filled with a cloud, so that the priests could not stand to minister because of the cloud, for the glory of the Lord filled the house of God.
> II Chronicles 5:11-14

Here we find not only the tremendous music ministry under the direction of Asaph, Heman, and Jeduthun leading the people in music that was true worship, but we also find God himself responding to this sacrifice of worship in such an overwhelming manifestation of his presence that they could not even continue the service.

Music ministry requires leadership. In this respect, worship today is no different from worship in the Old Testament. It is a sacrifice of praise unto God. Much of our worship today depends on the proper usage of music just as it did in David's time. More important than the musical expertise of a given minister is the comprehensive understanding of the biblical role of music in the life of his congregation. Just as David internalized these concepts and instilled them in the appointed leadership, so our ministers need to have sufficient understanding to generate proper direction and usage for the specialized leaders. Nor is mere musical expertise on the part of the music leaders adequate. They, too, must embody an understanding of the biblical function of music with their congregation. Just as the musicians in the Old Testament frequently led the congregation in worship, so must our musicians be capable of leading the people. Leading people in worship involves more than just the ability to lead a song. It is leading the people in a sacrifice of praise to God and engendering the proper response that the corporate assembly will respond in the same manner. It is the responsibility and privilege of all who would aspire to lead in music ministry.

Finally, the leaders of music ministry in Scripture had a responsibility to teach. Music education has been a part of the church since the Old Testament. It was through their ministry of teaching that music could be perpetuated as an integral part of worship. It was because of the teaching that biblical music is always characterized as being "skillful." Church leadership that seeks to build its music ministry on the scriptural model must take into consideration the aspect of providing music education. In the Old Testament there was an active training program for both children and adults. Training of the children was a requirement for musical leadership, but training for adults was equally important. Adulthood did not exempt anyone from this part of the ministry. Music ministers who neglect their responsibility in training others deny their biblical job description. The structure and methodology of this instruction will be investigated in our next section.

MUSIC AND SPECIALIZED PARTICIPATION

The Scriptures we have examined point out clearly that in addition to designated leadership, there were appointed singers and instrumentalists—musicians from the tribe of Levi. Just as it was essential for David to delegate leaders for the good of the people, so it was imperative that leadership establish a specialized group set apart for service and training in the ministry of music. Without these appointed singers and instrumentalists, music would never have achieved such heights in the worship, education, and evangelism of the people. Several characteristics merit examination.

First, *appointment meant focus.* No longer were these members of the priestly tribe groping around trying to find their avenue of service. Nor did they have to perform a variety of functions to merit their place within the priestly tribe. Their ministry became their primary concern in individual development and corporate usage. A variety of musical expressions were available to those appointed. Vocally there was opportunity for *solos.* David was a soloist, as was Chenaniah, and all the other priests who led the people in singing. The soloist frequently sang the musical phrase to the congregation and then had them repeat it, as discussed in chapter 2. We have one possible example of a *duet*—the victory song of Deborah and Barak. We know that *small ensembles* were used for various functions, for I Samuel 10:5 says:

> Afterward you will come to the hill of God where the Philistine garrison is; and it shall be as soon as you have come there to the city, that you will meet a group of prophets coming down from the high place with harp, tambourine, flute, and a lyre before them, and they will be prophesying.

All this was in addition to the *large choirs*—possibly a large mixed chorus for certain services, and possibly divided into men's and women's sections for use as antiphonal choirs.

Then there were opportunities for service on the instruments. There were three categories of instruments. First were the wind instruments, including, as we have mentioned, the trumpets. Also included were the *shofar* or ram's horn, used to signal the people, especially in warfare, and the *halil*, probably a double-pipe wind instrument with one pipe being melodic and one pipe drone. Then there were the stringed instruments—the harp, the lute, and the lyre. Finally, there were percussion instruments—cymbals, tambourines, and the drum *(tof)*, which was a shallow round-frame instrument most frequently played by women.

Second, *appointment meant discipline*. Appointment as a musician undoubtedly entailed hours of diligent rehearsals, for the repertoire of the Hebrews was vast. Because the Hebrews did not have a system of musical notation, all music had to be taught by rote. Although the form of ancient psalmody was fairly standard, slight melodic and rhythmic variations had to be taught and thoroughly practiced before the beautiful unison between the instrumentalists and the singers depicted in II Chronicles 5 could be achieved. Undoubtedly the use of hand symbols was utilized since they had no written notation, and the ancient hieroglyph for "song" is "hand." Nevertheless, without the standardization of written score, continuous repetition and rehearsal were essential before music could reach the standard of excellence required for public worship.

Third, *appointment meant responsibility*. It was the responsibility of each appointed musician to train his children in worship music. It was the children of these appointed musicians that formed the great children's choirs of the Old Testament. In fact, the appointment of singers and instrumentalists is only noted the first time it happened. After that, the appointment became inherited. We find this structure clearly outlined in I Chronicles where David and his commanders set apart for service Asaph, Heman, and Jeduthun and their children. Scripture lists the sons of each of these men, and then says:

> All these were the sons of Heman, the king's seer to exalt him according to the words of God, for God gave fourteen sons and three daughters to Heman. All these were under the direction of their father to sing in the house of the Lord, with cymbals, harps and lyres, for the service of the house of God. Asaph, Jeduthun and Heman were under the direction of the king. And their number who were trained in singing to the Lord, with their relatives, all who were skillful, was 288. And they cast lots for their duties, all alike, the small as well as the great, the teacher as well as the pupil.
> I Chronicles 25:5-8

We know then that children's choirs and instrumental ensembles were an integral part of the responsibility of the musicians, and that these groups performed publicly in praise to God. We also should note that their training was to such an extent that even the children were regarded as skillful.

Even after the Babylonian captivity, when the music of the Israelites became virtually dormant, Ezra numbers the population this way: "The whole assembly numbered 42,360, besides their male and female servants, who numbered 7,337; and they had 200 singing men and women" (Ez. 2:64-65). And in Nehemiah, when they are preparing to dedicate the wall, we read:

> Now at the dedication of the wall of Jerusalem they sought out the Levites from their places, to bring them to Jerusalem so that they might celebrate the dedication with gladness, with hymns of thanksgiving and with songs to the accompaniment of cymbals, harps, and lyres. So the sons of the singers were assembled from the district around Jerusalem.
> *Nehemiah 12:27-28*

Nehemiah goes on to describe the antiphonal choirs, but takes great care to establish the genealogy of those with musical instruments as being descendants of Asaph.

Finally, *appointment meant recognition.* The concentration of energy, discipline, and responsibility merited the musicians a place of recognition in ancient Jewish culture. Frequently the musicians led the army into battle. The musicians led the processional for the return of the Ark of the Covenant. They led the ceremonies at the dedication of the wall. They led in the dedication of the Temple. Their public ministry was recognized as a prominent part of the religious life of the entire assembly.

The New Testament abolishes the "caste" or "tribal" system in terms of priestly function. Hebrews 4-10 teaches that Jesus Christ has become our great high priest, offering once and for all a sacrifice for our sin, and sitting at the right hand of God daily making intercession for all. The sacrifice of Christ, therefore, opens the opportunity of spiritual leadership to all. We all have access to God, and thus are candidates for service.

The problem today arises when individuals or churches regard this open opportunity as license for lack of focus, discipline, responsibility, and recognition. On the contrary, the New Testament standards of acceptable service were just as demanding as those of the Old Testament. Paul enjoins us in Romans 12:1 to present our entire personhood as a living sacrifice, which he defines as our "spiritual service of worship." Too many times the designation "volunteer" choir or "volunteer" director has connoted something less than excellent because volunteers are seen as "less than professional." And too many times, volunteers do not demand of themselves the concentrated focus, discipline, or responsibility that is necessary for their ministry to be acceptable in the sight of God and recognized in the eyes of the people.

Children's choirs that become the "proving ground" for mediocre leadership, or that merely operate as "ornamentation" in performance are in contradiction to the biblical model.

Mature music ministry necessitates diligence on the part of its leadership as well as its participants—whether full-time music minister, sanctuary or children's choir director; adult or children's choir member. Music ministry in the church can never achieve the biblical prominence given to it without a portion of the people set apart for such ministry. Congregational music, while being extremely important to the life of the congregation, was never intended to take the place of the specialized music ministry.

Sanctuary choirs, festival choirs, children's choirs, small ensembles, orchestras, instrumental ensembles—all have their validity in Scripture. The choir director, the instrumental director, the children's choir director, the minister of music—all find their roots in the Bible. But all who would participate in this high calling must be aware of the biblical standard—focus, discipline, responsibility, and recognition.

MUSIC AND CONGREGATIONAL PARTICIPATION

Many problems arise in church music from limited perspective of proper biblical structure. These problems have perpetuated themselves throughout history, as we shall see in the next chapter. Many churches that have majored in music as a ministry of specialized participants have prohibited their congregations from participation because those who were specially trained were the only ones whose music

37

was regarded as suitable. Such a posture is incompatible with our scriptural model.

While one aspect of music in the church necessitates specialized involvement, another aspect of church music is equally essential to the life of the congregation—congregational music. Without congregational participation, worship becomes only an act of leadership and mere "spectator sport" for the congregation. Scripture clearly teaches that worship is an individual as well as a corporate act. We have already established the role that music plays in worship. To deny congregational participation in music not only distorts worship from an expression of participation to an act of performance, but it prevents the congregation from truly experiencing worship—the most necessary aspect of the learning process.

We found in our discussion of psalm singing in chapter 2 that direct psalmody was quickly replaced by responsorial psalmody because congregational participation was seen as essential not only in true worship, but in the education of the assembly. The easiest way to have the congregation memorize the Scriptures and learn the truths of Jehovah was to have them sing them.

Evidence seems to indicate that music became such a core ingredient of the Jewish educational structure that by the time of David and Solomon, most of the populace was educated musically to some degree and could demonstrate some skill as singers. What a tremendous testimony to have the song of the Lord not only sung by the "paid professionals" but written upon every heart in the nation of Israel! As a nation they could experience:

> Sing for joy to God our strength. . .
> For it is a statute for Israel,
> An ordinance of the God of Jacob.
> Psalm 81:1, 4

CONCLUSION

Scripture's model for the structure of a proper ministry is comprehensive. Departure from this model invalidates our purpose. Alignment with this model insures fulfillment of biblical purpose and will contribute significantly to worship, education, and evangelism in our churches.

The biblical structure requires that pastors and worship leaders fully understand the role of music in the life of the church. Not only must these individuals understand music, but they must insure its proper usage and administration first by example. Courses on philosophy of music in the local church need to be included in seminaries and Bible colleges as requirement for all who pursue the pastorate. If music is to achieve its purpose, it can only happen as pastors and church leaders are taught the biblical principles. Music was part of the training of the prophets—and it wasn't because they didn't have enough good musicians. It was because music was regarded as an essential in worship. Omitting such courses from pastoral preparation is a case of over-specialization, limiting perspective and diminishing effectiveness.

Then the clergy must try to appoint qualified music leaders. These leaders should demonstrate an understanding of the biblical role of music in the church and be highly skilled in their ability to lead the congregation and to teach. Perhaps the wisest policy is to appoint one music minister as "chief," who is responsible to the pastor in terms of philosophy and practice, and then various specialized leaders under the minister of music.

The responsibility of leadership to constantly be involved in teaching as well as leading helps multiply the ministry. Churches that see no growth in terms of addition or multiplication are usually neglecting this principle.

In addition, a music department structured according to the biblical model will recognize music as a ministry that merits the "setting apart" a portion of its congregation for specialized music service. Churches that allow no time in their program for choir rehearsals, instrumental ensemble rehearsals, children's choir rehearsals, and music education programs are in actuality preventing the development of a biblically structured music department. While it is obvious that many churches simply do not have the personnel, at least initially, to structure this extensive kind of program, they do have a responsibility to lay the proper foundation: developing leadership that can lead the people, training a small group willing to focus their energies on a musical ministry, and forming a children's music education and training program.

Persons willing to submit themselves to diligent training and consistent service deserve the recognition of the congregations they serve. Church musicians operating in accordance with biblical structure need to be recognized as ministers and worship leaders in their own right, not mere "music directors." Faithful choir members who devote their skill and service year after year are just as deserving of the designation of "minister" as those who are the leaders over them.

Children's music ministry is founded in Scripture. It is the responsibility of the most capable leadership—the most skilled in music. The purpose is outlined as skillful participation in worshiping the Lord in song, and training in all elements of skillful musicianship. Its purpose is closely aligned with the overall ministry of music in the church—not a tangent. Children's choirs that are subjected to mediocre leadership because of unwillingness on the part of the skilled, or graded choir programs that move through the year "from one performance to the next" with the associated performance-oriented rehearsals, deny their biblical validity. And those children's music programs that seek to exist without instilling diligence, discipline, and responsibility contribute nothing in establishing the biblical standard for acceptable ministry.

Music is a special function. Our leadership must understand this. Our schedules and programs must allow for it. But our response must merit it. The price of ministry was never designed to be cheap.

Finally, our music structure must incorporate the congregation. Ours is not a function of performance but of participation. The responsibility of the skilled is two-fold: to sing to the Lord, and to lead the people. Without congregational participation, biblical purpose becomes short-circuited and without meaning. Scripture is clear. Music ministry is an all-encompassing ministry—leadership, specialized participants, and congregation.

1. David Breed, *The History and Use of Hymns and Hymn-Tunes*. (Chicago: Fleming Revell Company, 1903), p. 14.

2. *Ibid.*, p. 13.

4
The Development
of Biblical Music

You shall therefore impress these words of mine on your heart
and on your soul. . . . And you shall teach them to your sons,
talking of them when you sit in your house and when you walk
along the road and when you lie down and when you rise up.
Deuteronomy 11:18-19

THERE IS AN OLD SAYING that those unwilling to learn from
history are doomed to repeat it. Church music history is no
exception. After examining the biblical model of music's
function, type, and structure, we can now trace the development of its practice through the centuries of the church.

Our purpose is not to present an extensive discourse on
church music history. That has been done by others listed in
the bibliography following this chapter. Our purpose here is
to look at the various functions, types, and structures of
music and observe the periods in which they flourished, or
were perhaps nonexistent. In so doing we will learn valuable
lessons in how to achieve and maintain spiritual health in
our church music programs.

THE DEVELOPMENT OF PSALMODY

Three major concerns faced the early Christians. As long
as Christ had been on earth, his followers looked directly to
him for direction. It was not until he gave his disciples their
post-ascension instructions that they had the full responsibility to take his message through Jerusalem, Judea, Samaria,
and all parts of the world. Thus, their first concern was
establishment of the church—organizing the followers of
Christ into groups of believers, instructing new converts,

41

and establishing them in local churches. Only as the church gathered and organized itself could it hope to survive the years until Christ would return.

The early church found itself in a culture dominated by the Roman emperor. The early Christians' second concern was maintaining their commitment to worship the one true God and to accept the authority of Christ alone, which was in complete opposition to the required allegiance to the state.

> The outward battle was fought on the technical issue of offering sacrifice to the genius of the emperor. . . . Historians have often remarked that the worst enemies of the Faith were the best of the Roman emperors. . . . The genius of Rome . . . was incompatible with Christianity. The Church could no more give allegiance to a state than it could burn incense to an emperor. The Christian could no more admit a philosophy of self-sufficiency than he could tolerate the image of the emperor on its altar. And so, while the worst of the emperors persecuted for vanity, the best of them persecuted for an ideal; and whether the persecution was of the one kind or the other, the Church met it defiantly and victoriously.[1]

The third concern of the early church was heresy. Gnosticism and Arianism were prevalent among so-called Christians. The Gnostics (from the Greek gnosis or "knowledge") stressed that people were saved through a mystical, secret knowledge. While they viewed all creation as evil, they believed that certain individuals destined for salvation had "sparks of divinity." Christ was sent to bring these special people redemption, in the form of this secret knowledge of themselves, their origin, and their destiny.[2] The Arians, on the other hand, believed that "the Son (Jesus) was essentially different from his Father. He did not possess by nature or right any of the divine qualities of immortality, sovereignty, perfect wisdom, goodness and purity. He did not exist before he was begotten by the Father."[3]

The challenge was incredible. But the early Christians met the challenge. And music played a significant part.

Paul's epistles and other early documents provide written evidence of the vital part that music played in the early church. We know that congregational singing of the psalms was a regular practice, both in the synagogue and by the early Christians, and by the end of the fourth century we have the *Apostolic Constitutions,* which prescribes specific psalms for the two daily services. Weekday mornings they sang Psalms 100; 141; 1; 63; 46; 71; and 93. Evening Psalms were 91; 134; and 4. Sunday services included Psalms 34; 92; 93; 95; 133; 136; 1; 100; 63; and 148-150. We also know that extensive psalm singing was an ingredient in private devotional life.

Why did the early Christians engage themselves in such extensive psalmody? While all critics agree that the psalms were held in the highest esteem and should be sung by all Christians, they differ in their opinions as to why this was true. Some theorize that they maintained this Jewish practice because it stressed a "new spirit" in old prayers. Others quote the therapeutic value of psalmody in terms of strengthening the inner person for times of difficulty and healing the wounds of life. Still others view psalm singing as a strong unifying force in a culture that was fragmented by many differing strains of Christianity. Psalm singing involved congregational participation—recognized as an extremely important factor, for it brought the people to unity in praise, and the "well-established textual and musical tradition served as regulators and teachers in the turbulent spiritual upheavals that preceded the fourth and fifth centuries."[4]

Thus we see that psalm singing significantly equipped the early church in meeting its first two challenges. First and foremost, it served to help the church establish itself. It brought together twice daily a group of believers for corporate praise to God—worship that expressed laud and adoration, thanksgiving, petition, and dedication. In so doing, it not only fulfilled their commandment to sing to the Lord, but it also equipped the person with courage and strength to face the difficulties of persecution (Ps. 46).

The next period in history that was to be significantly affected by psalm singing was the sixteenth century. The intervening centuries had witnessed a decline in congregational psalm singing. In A.D. 313, the Edict of Milan established Christianity as the official religion of the Roman empire. This end of persecution produced many positive results for church music. The position of cantor (the chief

43

soloist, and the forerunner of our present-day minister of music) became established. Boys' choirs began to spread throughout western Europe. A singing school (*Schola Cantorum*) was established in Rome for the training of church musicians. Pope Gregory I systematized much of the music that had heretofore been passed down orally. This well-organized collection of melodies that were assigned to different days and hours of services are designated by historians as "Gregorian chant," which stands in history as one of the most significant contributions to church music. Music developed from single-line melodies (monophonic music) to many parts singing complex independent melodies (polyphony). More emphasis was given instrumental music, especially that of the organ.

But while all this progress was occurring on one hand, there was regression on another. Latin, while becoming the official language of the church, was no longer the common language of the people. The religious leaders developed an ornate system of patriarchs, priests, bishops, and deacons—which, instead of always representing the people, began to exert great control over the church—both in liturgy and music. As the centuries passed, the gulf between the common people and the church leaders widened. Without congregational participation in psalm singing, the knowledge of the Scriptures vanished from the common parishioner and became available only to the clergy. Worship became an experience limited to clerical participation, with the congregation acting as spectators. With the absence of the people lifting their hearts in praise to God, the result was a lack of unity of purpose and penetration of scriptural truth into daily life. The people no longer felt the direct access to God in praise and prayer, but were prevented from participating in all areas of the church life.

In direct reaction to this came John Calvin (a contemporary of Martin Luther). Calvin's theology centered on Scripture and the sovereignty of God. His strong philosophy of music resembled his theology—man's responsibility to worship God demanded congregational singing of the divine praises. He felt that texts should be in the "vulgar tongue"—or the vernacular—because without understanding there was no edification. He also demanded musical modesty, which meant all music to God should be unaccompanied—although this was more because of man's evil abuses than inherent evil on the part of the instruments.[5]

Actually, metrical versions of psalmody in the sixteenth century began with Clement Marot of France, the court-poet to King Francis I.

Marot began to versify the psalms in 1533. Thirty of them were in circulation in manuscript form in 1537, and became the fashion of the hour. The king and his court sang them to ballad tunes, and from France they spread to adjoining countries. Their subsequent publication, in 1542, brought upon Marot the persecution of the Roman authorities and he fled to Geneva. Thence his psalmody spread through the Protestant world, and set the example for the host of versifiers who followed.[6]

It was while in Geneva that Marot met Calvin, who immediately recognized his talent and commissioned him to complete his psalter. But Marot died a year later, after completing only nineteen additional psalms. However, the work was completed by Louis Bourgeois, and in 1562 the *Genevan Psalter* was published—a task of monumental significance for church music history. In the first year alone there were twenty-five editions, and in the following hundred years, there were over 170 subsequent editions. Several of these tunes are still used today—most notably "Old Hundredth." Other psalters were published in Europe, most notably England and Scotland, but they will not be separately discussed here, as their effect in returning the Scriptures to the knowledge of the people, returning worship to the vernacular, and uniting the people in praise were common to all. "Take it for all in all, it is doubtful if any book of praise—the original Psalms alone excepted—has ever had so important a mission or exercised so great an influence."[7]

It is interesting to note that the first book published in America was a psalter—*The Bay Psalmist*. Prior to its publication, the colonies had used the "Ainsworth Version," which was printed in 1612 by Puritan refugees in Holland. Again, the desire for religious freedom was characterized by the use and publication of a psalter.

History teaches us that psalm singing is vital in congregational worship. The opportunity for the people to express praise to God in their own language and reaffirm the truths of Scripture is essential. God demands worship—and not just from the elite, the priesthood, or the musically trained. His command was for "everything that hath breath" to praise the Lord. Not even the magnificent music of the golden age of polyphony could satisfy this need. Just as the Israelites joined in a song of victory after their deliverance from Egypt, and the people cried "Hosanna, blessed is He that cometh in the name of the Lord" at the triumphal entry in Jerusalem, we must acknowledge people's right for musical expression to God, or the "very stones would cry out."

Psalm singing belongs in our congregations today. And psalm singing belongs in our children's programs. There is no better way to learn Scripture, no better way to experience worship. Corporate singing of praises unto God is "an ordinance of the God of Jacob."

THE DEVELOPMENT OF HYMNODY

After Christ it became essential for music to not only point out the prophecies of his coming, but the fact of his birth, life, death, and resurrection. It became important to sing about his teaching. Christ's death opened the door spiritually to the Gentiles, and formed his new covenant—his bride—the church. Although psalm singing was an essential part of church life, it became equally important to develop music other than that of Jewish origin.

The most widely recognized early Christian hymns were:

1. "Gloria in Excelsis," also called "The Greater Doxology" or "Angelic Hymn" because its text was taken from the angels' song at Bethlehem. The hymn deals largely with the person of Christ as the "lamb of God which taketh away the sins of the world" and "sits at the right hand of God the Father."

2. "Gloria Patri," or "Lesser Doxology," which says "Glory be to the Father and to the Son and to the Holy Ghost. As it was in the beginning, is now, and ever shall be world without end. Amen."

3. "Ter Sanctus," which was based on Isaiah 6:3 and Revelation 4:8, "Holy, holy, holy, Lord God Almighty, who was, and is, and is to come."

4. "Hallelujah," which for centuries had been the response of the people to the call of praise by the priest or

46

cantor. With its text and form deeply rooted in responsorial psalmody, the priest would sing, "Praise ye the Lord," to which the people would respond, "The Lord's name be praised."

5. The "Benedicte," which was the song of the three Hebrew children—a paraphrase of Psalm 48.

6. The "Nunc Dimittis," from the words of Simeon in Luke 2:29, "Lord, now lettest thou thy servant depart in peace. . . ." and was sung as the evening hymn.

7. The "Magnificat," which was Mary's response to the angel's annunciation in Luke 1:46ff.

8. The "Te Deum," or "Te Deum Laudamus," a hymn of praise to God, still sung today by denominations around the world.

9. The "Benedictus," which was the song of Zacharias at the birth of his son, John, recorded in Luke 1:68.[8]

Although each of these hymns was based on scriptural texts, it is important to notice the increased importance of New Testament Scriptures and emphasis on Christ.

But what about hymns that evolved from poetic and extrabiblical texts? It is important to recall the third cultural situation facing the early Christian church—the battle against the heresy of the Gnostics and the Arians. Understanding this challenge is important because it was initially the Gnostics and the Arians who were the most prolific hymn writers. They viewed hymn composition and singing as a primary means of propagating their views. To add to their subtlety, they "wrote hymns in imitation of the psalms, but with Gnostic additions."[9] It wasn't until the fourth century that there began to be a concerted effort to adopt a suitable body of Christian hymns. Up until this time these Gnostic hymns had gone unchallenged because persecution made many of the church activities clandestine. As a result, by the time Constantine legalized Christianity and they could publicly confront these sects, the Gnostic hymns not only outnumbered those considered "suitable," but they were far more familiar to the people.

It was Ephraim Syrus, a gifted poet and theologian, who saw hymn composition and participation as the most formidable way to refute the dangerous heretical disputes that divided the church. For this reason, his hymns had a strong

47

didactic, apologetic, and homiletic nature.[10]

The church split into two divisions after the political capital was moved from Rome to Constantinople. The western half of the empire still looked to Rome for church leadership, and the eastern half to Constantinople. Each branch developed its own personality and ethnic cultural traits. The hymn singing of the Eastern church didn't immediately transfer to the Western church, but when Ambrose was elected bishop of Milan in 374, following an Arian bishop, he was the first to introduce community hymn singing in the church, and at least four Latin hymns are credited to him.

The following is one of Ambrose's hymns. Two different translations are given. (Variations in translation are not limited to versions of the Bible!)

Maker of all things, God most high,
Great ruler of the starry sky,
Who, robing day with beauteous light,
Hast clothed in soft repose the night.

We thank thee for the day that's gone;
We pray thee for the night come on;
O help us sinners as we raise
To thee our votive hymn of praise.

Christ with the Father ever one,
Spirit! the Father and the Son,
God over all, the mighty sway,
Shield us, great Trinity, we pray.
Translated by John D. Chambers

Creator of the earth and sky,
Ruling the firmament on high,
Clothing the day with robes of light,
Blessing with gracious sleep the night.

Day sinks; we thank thee for thy gift;
Night comes; and once again we lift
Our prayer and vows and hymns that we
Against all ills may shielded be.

Pray we the Father and the Son,
And Holy Ghost: O Three in One,
Blest Trinity, whom all obey,
Guard thou thy sheep by night and day.
Translated by Charles Biggs

48

It is especially important to notice the last stanza, in either translation, for there we find an excellent illustration of the use of this hymn to combat heresy—a calculated attack on the Arian leadership that had preceded Ambrose.

The "Gloria Patri" was mentioned earlier. In its original form it had only the first section, "Glory be to the Father and to the Son and to the Holy Ghost." The second section "As it was in the beginning, is now, and ever shall be world without end. Amen." was added later as a direct attack on Arianism.[11]

Thus we can see that the absence of substantial hymn singing at the beginning of the early Christian church may have helped allow heresy to infiltrate church life—both congregation and leadership. Conversely, it was hymn singing that led the attack on this improper teaching, at least as far as congregational involvement was concerned. It was congregational hymn singing that contributed significantly to the success of the early church in meeting its third challenge.

But fighting Arianism and Gnosticism were not the only purposes of Ambrose. He was equally concerned that there were hymns suitable for use in Christian worship in times of peace and contemplation. The custom of hymn singing in the evening had become entrenched in society (partly due to the struggle against the Arians).

> When the Arians were forbidden by the orthodox Emperor Theodosius (378-96) to hold public worship in Constantinople (the political capital), the Arians retorted by parading through the streets singing hymns. John Chrysostom organized rival processions of hymn-singers, and since these things took place at sunset, the custom of evening hymn-singing became either established or at least immeasurably strengthened in the Christian church.[12]

But Ambrose realized that while this struggle would be brought to an end, the practice of hymn singing had come to stay. He longed for texts that would edify the person as well as articulate the conflict. He longed for texts that would reinforce truth in the life of the individual regardless of outward circumstances.

Ambrose, therefore, composed and caused to be composed the

first of what we now call the "office hymns"—hymns prescribed to be sung at certain stages of the church's worship. These hymns are extremely simple, entirely objective, and non-controversial, and of the homely sort that wear well in constant use.[13]

The purpose of these hymns was praise and adoration and declaration of divine truth.

Unfortunately, while the allocation of proper hymns for the offices insured the use of hymns during the next several centuries, it did not insure congregational knowledge or participation. It was the Mass, and not the offices, that were designed as the public celebrations of worship, and the congregation had virtually no participation in the Mass. Also, because of controversies, music in the Mass was limited to scriptural chanting. The offices, on the other hand, were allowed to incorporate hymns, but they were regarded as the duty of the religious leaders and not the populace, so the peasants seldom attended. Tragically, personal expression of devotion had no place in the medieval church.

As we noted in our examination of psalmody, when musical expression of praise to God is taken away from the people, the church suffers devastating consequences. Worship was never designed as a "spectator sport" but was created by God to be an expression, first to himself, then to the people of God, and finally the world at large, of the truths of his divine person and his laws. The decline of hymnody created such spiritual malnourishment that the people became the pawns of the religious leaders—"cast about by every wind of doctrine"—and the religious leaders capitalized on the stranglehold.

It was into the dark picture that Martin Luther came as a bright light. Not only did he violently oppose the selling of indulgences for the absolution of sins, he believed in the priesthood of every believer and demanded congregational participation—most notably in hymn singing. In fact, just as the Arians had regarded hymn singing as the most effective means of propagating their heresy, Luther regarded hymn singing the most excellent method to provide the people with theological truth. Many of his statements verify his strong conviction of the power of music and the necessity for it to be understood and sung by the common people.

I truly desire that all Christians would love and regard as worthy the lovely gift of music, which is a precious, worthy, and costly treasure given mankind by God. The riches of music are so excellent and so precious that words fail me whenever I attempt to discuss and describe them. . . . In summa, next to the Word of God, the noble art of music is the greatest treasure in this world. It controls our thoughts, minds, hearts, and spirits.[14]

And in another place:

I am willing to make German psalms for the people, according to the example set by the prophets and ancient fathers; by this I mean that I am willing to prepare spiritual songs (hymns) in order that the Word of God may be conserved among the people through singing also.[15]

Of course, his most noted hymn is "A Mighty Fortress Is Our God." In addition to his own hymns, he diligently sought the assistance of other notable musicians and poets, most notably Johann Walther, to assist him in putting scriptural truths in the vernacular. Luther's first hymnal was published in 1524, and contained only eight hymns—four by Luther. This hymnal was stated for use in church and home. Luther was a strong advocate of learning hymns at home so that texts would be reinforced in the daily life of the believer. He also incorporated them into this childhood education by teaching extensive hymnody in his parochial schools. Thus, the significance of Martin Luther was not limited to the theological societies of the day or retained within monastery walls—his influence infiltrated every aspect of his culture and changed the course of church history—and even human history, in that the truths of God's Word were once again returned to the people.

Isaac Watts, the father of English hymnody, once criticized the versification of psalms used in his church. A leader in the church challenged him to write something better if he did not like what was being used. Watts took up the challenge and wrote a new hymn for every Sunday until he had written over two hundred hymns. In keeping with his strong commitment to scriptural content, his most extensive work was a new versification of the Psalms—although his versions were characterized by a strong New Testament

51

flavor given to Old Testament poetry. He believed that his texts were "what David would have written if he had lived in the days of Christianity." For example, he took Psalm 72:

"Give the king Thy judgments, O God,
And Thy righteousness to the king's son."

and composed the hymn:

"Jesus shall reign where'er the sun
Does his successive journeys run."

However, his finest hymn, and perhaps one of the greatest in all church hymnody is "When I Survey the Wondrous Cross."

When I survey the wondrous cross,
   On which the Prince of glory died,
My richest gain I count but loss,
   And pour contempt on all my pride.

Forbid it, Lord! that I should boast,
   Save in the death of Christ, my God;
All the vain things that charm me most,
   I sacrifice them to his blood.

See, from his head, his hands, his feet,
   Sorrow and love flow mingled down;
Did e'er such love and sorrow meet,
   Or thorns compose so rich a crown?

His dying crimson, like a robe
   Spreads o'er his body on the tree;
Then I am dead to all the globe,
   And all the globe is dead to me.

Were the whole realm of nature mine,
   That were a present far too small;
Love so amazing, so divine,
   Demands my soul, my life, my all.

This magnificent statement combines theology, adoration, commitment, and much more in its few short verses, and its place in history is established by its wide usage in public worship and the fact that it has stood the test of time and still is one of our most significant hymns today. Watts lived during a time when hymns were strongly didactic in content, and his are no exception. They embody many of the foundational truths in Scripture and are just as essential in our Christian education as they were in the late seventeenth and early eighteenth centuries.

Any student of the eighteenth century, whether church-related or not, cannot miss the outstanding influence of Charles Wesley and his brother John upon this century. John has come to be known as the founder of Methodism and was known for his prose writings and his hymns, mostly translations from German. The more than six thousand hymns of Charles were, on the other hand, mostly original. Many of them are sung by evangelical denominations all over the world. Several of those most universal hymns are: "Jesus, Lover of My Soul," "Hark! The Herald Angels Sing," "Oh, For a Thousand Tongues to Sing," "Ye Servants of God, Your Master Proclaim," "Come Thou Long Expected Jesus," and "Love Divine All Loves Excelling."

While the Wesleys exhibited outstanding gifts at composition of original texts and tunes, their vast knowledge of ancient church hymnody coupled with their extensive travel placed them in a significant position in church music. Many of the ancient hymns they translated and revised. Realizing the tremendous worth these hymns had contributed in previous centuries, it was the Wesleys' desire to let their congregations experience these hymns. In 1735, the Wesleys visited America, and coincidentally met a group of twenty-six Moravians on the ship. This group had originated with John Huss, and after his torturous death, formed a small colony in Herrnhut, Germany. They were characterized by their enthusiastic hymn singing, and this musical expression of faith and worship deeply affected the Wesleys, so much so that John Wesley published a hymnal in America after their arrival. This first *Collection of Psalms and Hymns,* published in Charlestown, 1737, contained seventy hymns, some of which they had brought from England, and some of which were translated Moravian hymns. Ironically, though Charles Wesley later became known for his hymns, it was *A Collection of Psalms and Hymns,* by John Wesley, that became the first hymnal ever used in an Anglican church.

The following century reflected the expansion of the

Romantic movement. Conceptually, music followed the predominant characteristics of the other arts—a rejection of classical rigidity and the development of deep emotional expression. Hymn texts became much more personal. Melodies and harmonies reflected the emotional predominance of the great composers such as Beethoven. Examples of such hymns are: "In the Cross of Christ I Glory," "Just As I Am, Without One Plea," "Sun of My Soul, Thou Saviour Dear," and "Abide With Me."

In the 1830s, a group known as the "Tractarians"—followers of John Henry Newman, John Keble, and E. B. Pusey, and characterized by the wide distribution of pamphlets dealing with national apostasy, church history, and doctrine—made significant attempts to revitalize the Anglican church. They felt that this revitalization could best be accomplished by purification of its service. Thus they placed strong emphasis on the sacraments of the church, renewed use of the *Book of Common Prayer*, and in general returned to much of the Catholic liturgy that had prevailed during the medieval period. They contributed much to church hymnody—they recognized the values of many of the old hymn texts, but knew that their use in earlier centuries had been limited because of Latin texts, or lack of congregational participation, or both. As a result, they translated many hymns that are still widely used today. Some of the best examples are: "Jesus, the Very Thought of Thee," "O Come, O Come, Emmanuel," and "Praise to the Lord, the Almighty."

However, though there was significant revitalization, there also developed a chasm between the fine "liturgical hymns" and the personal "evangelical hymns."

> The Evangelical Hymn is inevitably the voice of the believer; the Liturgical Hymn is the voice of the worshipping church. The Evangelical Hymn deals primarily with inward experience; the Liturgical Hymn, even though expressive of common experience, relates it objectively to the hour of worship, the church season or occasion, the ordinance and sacrament. The Evangelical Hymn is free; the Liturgical Hymn closely articulated liturgical order, having its fixed place which determines its content.[16]

The greatest contribution of the Oxford Movement (as the Tractarians came to be known) was the compilation of a most influential hymnal, (Hymns Ancient and Modern) It became a national institution in England, and its influence has permeated the entire English-speaking world. "All subsequent hymnal compilers are debtors to this hymnal, for they have reprinted its liturgical hymns, copied its format, and maintained the marriages of many texts and tunes which appeared here for the first time together."[17] The total sales of this hymnal are beyond computation.

> The total sales since 1860 cannot be ascertained, for the publishers' records were destroyed in the war of 1939-45, but the hundred million mark was passed many years ago. If we say 150,000,000, we shall not be far wrong.[18]

"Of the 273 hymns in this collection, 131 were of English origin, 132 were Latin translations, and 10 were German translations. Only 12 of the English hymns were new, 119 having been already in use."[19] We must observe then, that the new hymns of the nineteenth century were, for the most part, not accepted within the collection of the church hymnal. Their Romantic nature was viewed as less desirable than the more formal classical type.

Against this backdrop, we must mention the work of some nineteenth-century composers—Ira Sankey, Fanny Crosby, and P. P. Bliss. Ira Sankey wrote gospel hymns for evangelist Dwight L. Moody. Although it is not common knowledge, Sankey was preceded in his involvement with Moody by Philip Bliss, whose singing in Moody's services first made Moody aware of the tremendous value of music in his revival campaigns. One of Bliss' best-known songs was "Wonderful Words of Life." Sankey is remembered most for his "Ninety and Nine." While most of their songs have come under severe criticism from the music professionals and liturgical churches, we should remember that the great revivalists of the nineteenth century were not concerned with building a worshiping church. Their purpose was to reach converts. Their influence was, for the most part, outside the church in large crusade-type meetings in which the large percentage of the audience was unchurched—and in many cases uneducated. Thus, most of their songs presented simple texts and melodies that made a strong appeal to the individual. The entire purpose of "The Ninety and Nine" was to get the listener to identify with the "one lost sheep." Many of these songs were written almost spontaneously to fit the need of the moment. Other times texts were supplied by other writers who were sympathetic to the work of the evangelists and would write with mass evangelism in mind.

Fanny Crosby, though blind from birth, was probably the most prolific gospel songwriter of the century, writing about 8,000 songs. She was a member of St. John's Methodist Episcopal Church in New York City, and many of her songs were written for congregational use there, such as "Jesus, Keep Me Near the Cross" and "To God Be The Glory." However, she also supplied texts for Sankey and others involved in mass evangelism. Her music was characterized by simplicity and personal experience.

The value of these songs must be established in terms of their audience. We established in chapter 1 that in worship, God was the audience. Thus, for worship, these songs are unsuitable—they were not written to be sung to God. But they are intended to communicate biblical truths on a personal level to those outside the Body of Christ. If evangelism is your purpose, the people's needs are the focus. Because of the central position the church for centuries held in society, it was possible to have men realize their need for redemption through the doctrinal preaching and hymn singing.

Ever since the industrial revolution, however, the church has lost its place as the focal point of society, and evangelism has had to move, for the most part, outside the church walls.

Hymns have been significant in worship and education since the days of the Old Testament. As we saw in chapter 1, biblical worship is an offering to God, is required by God, affirms God's character and man's position as his creation, and demands both intellect and emotion. We examined the nature of worship: praise, adoration, dedication, confession, and petition. We established education as the internalization of doctrine, the acceptance of reproof, the implementation of correction, and instruction in righteousness. Where in worship music God is the audience, in education music the audience is God's people.

To discard the gospel song, however, because it does not fit any of the above criteria is wrong. The Bible also presents music in a third way—as evangelism. And we must remember that scriptural perspective does not allow for priorital arrangement according to function—all three are essential to the life of the church. Those who tenaciously regard the gospel song as worship need to reexamine the scriptural characteristics of worship. But those who relegate them to the cultural gutters need to remember Christ's practice of reaching sinners many times by meeting their needs. Gospel songs, likewise, try to apply the gospel to the needs of people.

The problem comes when after conversion, the individual still satisfies his spiritual development with songs that reflect only personal experience. Tragedy and spiritual "ill-health" result when we deny the biblical injunction to "sing to the Lord." The believer is commanded to "grow up into Christ." While it is valid to express personal experience, we can never reduce God's greatness, holiness, and omnipotence to our personal experience. We have a responsibility to sing out of knowledge—the knowledge of the truth of the Word of God—a knowledge that far surpasses our finite humanness.

Finally, we must be careful about using archaic texts. Throughout history the greatest church musicians constantly kept before them the need for the texts of the hymns to be in the language of the people. Constant revision and translation were characteristic of Ambrose of Milan, Martin Luther, Isaac Watts, and John and Charles Wesley. All of them realized that if the people could not understand the words, there was no edification. While many of the hymns of the Reformation and following centuries can still be understood by church congregations, we do not need to hold "sacred" a text simply because it is old. Reediting and revising should be constantly at work within the field of church music. To do so will help us express in fresh, meaningful language the biblical truths that have stood from the beginning of time.

THE DEVELOPMENT OF SPIRITUAL SONGS

Spiritual songs developed a completely different personality than psalms and hymns. In psalms, the syllabic and syntactic structure were the controlling elements. In hymns, the metrical poetry became a governing aspect. The spiritual

57

song was an ecstatic expression of joy. The singer was free to improvise his enthusiastic response.

At times this enthusiastic response was designed for congregational use—when they would sing "Hallelujah" following the chanting of a Scripture passage. It was especially helpful with more "primitive" audiences who did not know the psalms, but nevertheless needed to participate even if only by affirming the message with an "Amen" or "Praise God" or "Alleluia." The word *Alleluia* (or *hallelujah*) is a composite of two words—*Hallel*, meaning "praise," and *jah* or "jahweh," which is the Hebrew word for God.

At other times it was sung by a soloist—many times a highly skilled musician—who sang his ornate musical expression initially as an interlude to another musical type—a psalm or a hymn. In time, however, these interludes developed into such extensive pieces that they dwarfed the surrounding psalm or hymn, and they became independent songs in their own right. This was given the title "Jubili."

This Jubili—a wordless song of joy—took the musical form of a melisma, an ornate group of notes sung to one syllable. We have many examples of melismas in later music, for example Handel's *Messiah*, where the vocal line sings these ornate melodic passages to one syllable to emphasize certain words. The practice of singing these extended musical phrases can be traced back to the earliest times, and in fact in pagan cultures were frequently regarded as a kind of magical incantation. Although not regarded as magical in Judaic culture, their effect was seen in engendering an emotional response rather than an objective result.

This type of music was considered to be the song of the angels, and human performance was regarded as imitation of the angelic hymns. The singing of these extended hallelujahs was considered indispensable to Jewish and New Testament worship, and frequently reflected the personality of the week or time of year. Weekday services employed less of the Jubili than did the Sunday services, and celebrations of Easter, Pentecost, and Epiphany were more elaborately embellished than regular Sundays. When Constantine ended the persecution of the Christians and established Christianity as the religion of the Roman Empire, the Jubili became one of the single most important elements in the church assembly. We also know that these ecstatic expressions varied greatly because of ethnic and cultural factors.

Some of the most important forms of the musical liturgy of all churches belong to this category. The remarkable divergences between the various types, with respect to their literary and musical development, cannot be explained from the liturgical aspect alone. It was here that the genius of the respective population, its national and religious character, asserted itself. No less important was the genius of the various languages of the liturgies which created their own structures, their poetical as well as musical forms. In short, here, more than in any other sphere, the ethnic and regional forces determined the evolution of the psalmodic melismatic types.[20]

Apparently it was vital to Christians through the years to include a type of music that allowed for spontaneous enthusiastic expressions that were suited culturally for the people participating. Even after the Jubili became an independent form, it did not conform to the genuine hymnic structure, but maintained the nature of a free poem.

Functionally these songs, and others developed as time went on, served to emphasize and intensify the meaning of the service—whether a Scripture lesson or sermon. Certain melodies even came to be associated with certain types of texts so that a composer could take an already established melody, vary it slightly, and adjust the text for the occasion.

The composer did not have to compose an entirely different tune . . . ; his task was rather that of a modest artisan who wished to add to an admired model something which seems permissible to him as an intensification . . . or a small variation.[21]

During the medieval period, much of the ornate melismatic song moved to the professional singers and away from congregational participation, as it did in the other forms of music as well. In the Mass, the public worship service on Sundays, the music was characteristically performed by members of the *Schola Cantorum*, the singing school established in Rome during the fifth century for the training of church musicians. However, the music of the Offices, the daily services designed for prayers for the people, was characteristically simple. Instead of being performed by the trained musicians, this music was designed for the secular priests or monks with no musical training. They usually employed a limited vocal range, stepwise motion, few melodic jumps, and were short—all basic elements of music meant to be performed by average clerics or laymen.

This dualism in practice (professional versus laity) and style (ornate versus simple), stemming from the Jubili illustrates the tension between formal music construction and spontaneous melodic improvisation. Thus this music of the spirit—the spiritual songs—developed into two streams— one rooted in professional artistry and the other in stylized folklore—each with its own unique validity and function. The music of artistry survived throughout the centuries because of its perpetuation through the musically trained, and eventually through music notation. On the other hand, the music of the folk idiom, although enthusiastic in nature, was frequently short-lived because of its tie with societal needs and modes of expression. Those that did survive did so through oral tradition. Not until music notation became widespread and accessible to the common people do we find many of these songs in written documents.

In our section on hymnody, we mentioned the Moravians and their profound effect upon the Wesleys. While it is true that Moravians are best known for their hymnody, they also employed much spontaneous folklore music in their evangelistic efforts. The Moravians were part of the Pietistic movement—dedicated to returning the church to strict piety. They created a vast number of songs intended solely for temporary congregational use. Their source material was twofold—medieval sacred songs and folk songs. Zinzendorf, a wealthy count on whose estate the Moravians settled in Herrnhut, Germany, and eventual leader of the movement, gave the community the "hours of song." These were special songs assigned to different hours of the day—similar to the Offices initiated by Ambrose in the fourth century.

Some of Zinzendorf's remarks suggest that singing and the hours of song were to him the focal points of spiritual and congregational life. He felt that they were ways to a genuine expression of enthusiastic pietistic faith and therefore a measure of the spiritual condition of the congregation. He said of the songs that they were "the best method to bring God's truth to the heart and to preserve it there."[22]

His spontaneous improvisation of songs for the people is best understood in his own words:

> During public prayer hours, however, I first have a familiar song recited before [the sermon]. After it, however, if I do not find a song in the hymnal that I would like to have sung to emphasize the subject matter of my sermon to the audience and to offer it to the Savior as a prayer, I invent a new song of which I knew nothing before and which will be forgotten as soon as it has served its purpose.[23]

It is significant to note the missionary results of Moravian music. Their melodies penetrated eleven languages and eventually spread around the world. Not only did they provide a solid structure of hymnody, but they employed music that spoke enthusiastically and emotionally to the needs and experiences of the people. These songs intensified the spoken word and established an identity with the listener, transforming the objective message to a subjective personal experience.

The fact that this type of music has always been a part of Judeo-Christian worship is a matter of historical record. It was most certainly a part of Davidic expression, New Testament expression, Medieval expression, Reformation and post-Reformation expression, and is still prevalent today, especially in Negro spirituals.

Why is this music important in the life of the church—both corporately and individually? Music not only has the power to aid learning and internalize doctrine, it also has the power to bring out an emotional response. This is neither degrading to music nor mankind. It is, rather, a beautiful illustration of God's creative genius in creating such a gift that can significantly effect both the intellect and the emotions.

It should be observed that this particular type of music flourished to its greatest proportions during times of two other developments in the church: (1) when the musical expressions in the worship service became too ornate for congregational participation and were reserved for professional musicians, the language was not in the vernacular, ethnic and culture considerations were ignored, and public services did not allow for enthusiastic audience response, and (2) during times of great evangelism, when the gospel was taken outside the church walls and presented directly to the people.

Perhaps this is where the gospel songs should actually be categorized. Just as many of the spiritual songs throughout history have been composed on the spot for a specific purpose, so has the gospel song. Just as the medieval type employed a limited vocal range, stepwise motion, few melodic jumps, and brief simplistic style—so the average lay person could easily sing it—so does the gospel song. Just as they were employed to intensify a certain point in the sermon or Scripture lesson, thereby creating an identity with the audience, so was the gospel song. Just as it has always been primarily viewed as an emotional expression, so is the gospel song.

> The gospel song is not a hymn of praise to be sung in worship with stateliness and dignity. A militant song, it was forged quickly in the heat of battle for the souls of men, and designed to produce an immediate evangelistic decision. That it was successful in this objective in the Dwight L. Moody meetings is a matter of historical record. . . . The gospel song appeared as an answer to a specific need. The need was for a popular religious song with which the people could find immediate emotional identification and in which they could express their religious experiences of the campfire meeting and the evangelistic campaign.[24]

The fact that music notation and publication has become so widespread has perpetuated many of these songs past their normal life span. For this reason, many people deny the worth of not only specific songs but this type of music as a whole. This is unfortunate. To castigate this type of music as a degenerative by-product of the Romantic era, when art, including music, was pitched at emotional extremes to create certain responses, seems to be naive. On the other hand, to place it alongside the artistic hymnody of the church is equally naive. We must remember that hymns are primarily concerned with foundational truth expressed in an artistic musical form that transcends generations. Hymn singing is an essential ingredient in worship, education, and edification. The spiritual song, on the other hand, focuses on experiences, and uses modes of expression that are contemporary—popular one generation, and outdated the next.

We must constantly remember that worship and expression to God has always maintained a dimension that was designed for the population at large. In God's design he created specialized functions, including those who were to specialize in music ministry. However, their function was best achieved in enhancing and enlarging congregational participation—not usurping it. While it is unnecessary, and perhaps undesirable, to tenaciously hold on to songs that were designed to fill a certain need at a certain time, it is equally damaging to exclude them from the musical expression of our people—children as well as adults. Undoubtedly, some of them will outlive others and find their place in music history. Many of them will not.

Scripture designates three types of music—psalms, hymns, and spiritual songs. Too many times music selection becomes a matter of personal preference rather than following the biblical pattern. Our generation is not the first to quibble over appropriate musical types. But we must remember that if we look only at our particular church, locale, or time in history, we are destined to become short-sighted in our perspective. In church history, two elements seem to reflect one another—theology and music. When psalm singing flourished, so did the unity in praise to God—the recognition of the person of God. When corporate worship declined, so did psalm singing. Hymn singing flourished when theological teaching and doctrinal understanding were emphasized. When hymns and doctrine began to wane, heresy infiltrated. When spiritual songs flourished, so did the enthusiastic emotional involvement and response of the people. When the teaching of the church became only an objective process, permeating neither the culture nor the needs of the individual it was designed to satisfy, spiritual songs tended to die out. Religion became an expression for the elite rather than an experience for the masses.

Church music has always sought a balance of expression.

When one type or another has been denied, sweeping reform has erupted. How much more beneficial it would be to chart a course based on the full biblical pattern and amplified by historical perspective, than to waste valuable time and creative energy swinging from one end of the pendulum to the other. We cannot hope to create healthy Christians "thoroughly furnished unto all good works," and healthy churches fulfilling the ministry of worship, education, and evangelism, by perpetuating musical prejudice—regardless at which end of the spectrum we find ourselves. The biblical pattern is clear. To all who follow, the rewards are innumerable.

DEVELOPMENT OF BIBLICAL STRUCTURE

In chapter 3 we spent extended time diagnosing biblical patterns for structure of music ministry—from specialized participants to music education for our children to congregational participation. Our observations of church music history would not be complete without some mention of how these structures developed throughout the centuries.

Church leadership played a significant role by understanding the ministry of music as foundational to its proper functioning. Pope Gregory and John Calvin, although separated by centuries, provided the dynamic leadership for the perpetuation of psalmody. Ephraim Syrus, Ambrose of Milan, and Martin Luther, all notable theologians of their day, spearheaded the development of hymnody. And it was the hymns of John and Charles Wesley that provided a legacy of the finest church hymns for generations to follow. It was under the monastic leadership and the clerics of the medieval world that the spiritual song verbalized the intensities of spiritual truth in an idiom that was culturally and ethnically determined. Count Zinzendorf and Dwight L. Moody—both leaders of an evangelistic movement, gave prominence to the spiritual song.

Just as some theologians have provided proper impetus for the development of church music, it must be noted that when leadership does not have a proper understanding of biblical perspective, church music can be significantly damaged. The bickering over the inclusion of non-scriptural texts—poetry based on scriptural truth, but not quoting an exact scripture—hindered the development of hymns and spiritual songs for centuries during the post-apostolic era. Legislation such as the Council of Laodicea in A.D 367, which prohibited congregational participation, began to move worship from the sphere of the corporate body to the realm only of the specialized clergy.

What should be the role of specialized music leaders and participants? Many people today feel that a specialized music ministry is superfluous. They are willing to let their music either operate without skilled leadership, or perhaps pass from one volunteer to another, or else include it as a small part of an overall job description. Some negate the place of a specialized choir, preferring to let the entire congregation serve as choir. In Scripture, however, as we saw in chapter 3, a role is given to those in specialized music ministry—both in leadership and participation. History further confirms this concept.

When music in the church has lacked the leadership of a skillful musician, fully competent as a spiritual leader and capable musician, able to lead the people, the choir, and provide training, it has become the pawn of preferential bias by those with musical opinions but little scriptural understanding. Then music degenerates to the least common denominator of the congregation.

It is essential that we realize that the role of those set apart as musical specialists to minister to the Lord and to the Lord's people is most accurately characterized as enhancing and not usurping. It is equally essential, however, that we not eliminate this vital ministry in the name of congregational expediency.

Choirs have the special ability to spend time learning new repertoire and then, through repeated use, teach it to the congregation. This is how the Hebrews in the Old Testament learned hymns. It has been a common technique of music instruction, until recent days when the plethora of hymnals and musical notation has placed an abundant repertoire in the hands of every churchgoer. And yet the tragedy is that in so many churches we are still afraid to try the new hymns in our hymnals—because we are afraid that no one will know them. How effective it would be to return to Old Testament and early church techniques where the choir teaches the congregation the Scripture lesson or central theme of the service by helping them learn a new hymn.

Without our specialized church musicians, church music would be a dirth rather than a wealth of biblical expression. To delegate this kind of responsibility to an already overworked pastor—who, regardless of musical expertise, cannot possibly give it the priority it deserves—or to designate it to some well-meaning soul who can only carry a tune and wave his arms and who needs to be "involved," will diminish music to something less than Scripture intended. While this does not mean that the answers to the problems of every small, struggling church is to hire a minister of music, it does mean that music needs to be approached with the same care and thorough examination that would be given any other area of vital church life.

Finally, we need to observe the development of music education within the church. All the previous background is basic for any aspect of music ministry. Certainly an understanding of biblical function, biblical type, and biblical structure are minimum essentials for any person exercising musical leadership. It was, however, the persuasion of King David in the Old Testament, the church musicians in the early centuries, Martin Luther in the sixteenth century, and countless others, that the most effective way of perpetuating not only the biblical philosophy but also the *practice* of church music was by providing an effective training program for children. Without a structure for implementation, all lofty concepts are limited to library shelves. A comprehensive music education program provides the most excellent structure for "practicing what we preach."

It was no accident that part of the primary responsibility of the most skilled music leaders in the Old Testament—Chenaniah, Asaph, Heman, and Jeduthun—was to teach music to those younger. This included music instruction in every dimension. Without a comprehensive training program, it would have been impossible for Israel's music ministry to achieve and maintain its God-given potential.

After the days of persecution of the Christians had ended, it was realized that the only way to restore music to its place of prominence in the operation of the church was through an extensive education for young children—most commonly boys. Thus the *Schola Cantorum* was founded and gave to all Europe a model for training young children as well as adults in music. It wasn't long until these schools were scattered throughout Europe.

Martin Luther was actively involved in children's music education. Not only was it included as part of his catechism curriculum, but Luther also helped his congregation learn new hymns by first teaching them to the children and then having them teach their parents at home. He also held rehearsals on Sunday afternoons for families to come and practice the new hymns. He was a strong advocate of hymn singing in family devotional life and knew that a solid music training program was vital for the extended life of the church.

And it has been the same in modern times. Psalm singing had been revitalized during the sixteenth century and the American colonies had initially participated vigorously in this type of musical expression. And yet because of the lack of books containing the melodies—and even more specifically—the ability of the people to read the tunes even if they had had access to them—psalm singing began to decline. Singing became limited to the familiar tunes, and as the number of familiar tunes became less and less, some churches completely eliminated psalm singing.

> The traditional practice of "lining out" the psalm added to this gradual decline. Because of the lack of hymnals to supply the entire congregation, a deacon was appointed to "line out" the psalm. He would read aloud a line or two, and then the congregation would join in singing that which had just been read. Little effort was made to establish a mutual agreement as to the key of the tune, and when the congregation joined in singing the words lined out by the deacon, everyone sang the tune in his own way, using his own pitch and tempo. Tunes were distorted until they became almost unrecognizable, and the breakdown of rhythmic structure reduced the tempo to the slowest possible movement.[25]

The only solution to this chaos was music education—teaching the people to sing properly and read musical notation. The movement was spearheaded by three reformers: John Tufts, who published a small collection, *An Introduc-*

67

tion to the Singing of Psalm-Tunes; Thomas Symmes, who contributed *The Reasonableness of Regular Singing, or Singing by Note;* and Thomas Walter, who wrote *The Grounds and Rules of Musical Experience.* All three publications appeared about 1720. These works gave rise to many church-sponsored singing schools. Although initially conceived to promote psalm singing, hymns and anthems were added as they began to be incorporated in the new tune books that were used. Churches would secure the services of a local music teacher who would hold the singing school in a variety of locations—all within easy access of the townspeople. They used taverns, schools, and any buildings that were made available to them. Eventually, attendance at these schools became socially advantageous—and it is these early singing schools that laid the foundation for community music societies such as the Boston Handel and Haydn Society.[26]

Lowell Mason, an outstanding musician of the early nineteenth century, served as the choir director of the Bowdoin Street Church in Boston, Massachusetts. Although his church choir received national recognition for the quality of its singing, Mason determined to improve music in both the choir and the congregation. To achieve his goal he began music classes for the children in his church and published *The Juvenile Psalmist, or The Child's Introduction to Sacred Music,* in 1829. In 1832, he expanded his goal to include all churches and founded the Boston Academy of Music. But his ambition did not stop there, and by 1838, he had successfully initiated the teaching of vocal music in the public schools of Boston in "preparation for making the praise of God glorious in families and churches."[27] It is most apparent that Mason's understanding of the God-given gift of music needed to penetrate all levels—the specialized musicians (the choir), the congregation, and then family units. His concept bears striking resemblance to the Old Testament. The method of achievement was the same—a comprehensive music education program for children.

A music education program is an integral part of biblical church music structure. It is there that philosophical concepts become living reality. It is there that the practices are hammered out and developed. It is in the childhood years that proper function and a balance of musical types can be experienced without inhibition or preconditioned prejudice.

This kind of musical development cannot be found in secular music education. We must provide for it in the church. The money available for quality music education in the public schools will undoubtedly become less and less during the next decade. It is time that the church resume the position it has always had—the music educator of the society. It can only promote a more intimate relationship between the church and the society in which it functions.

When approached from a biblical perspective, music can significantly affect the worship, education, and evangelism of our congregations, as well as the intellectual, emotional, and experiential development of the individuals to whom we minister. The opportunity has never been greater. The principles are powerful. The time has come to mobilize.

CONCLUSION

The first section of this book has attempted to develop a proper biblical perspective of music ministry in the church. We have examined music's functions: worship, education, and evangelism. We have scrutinized the three biblical types: psalms, hymns, and spiritual songs. And we have looked at the structure to put this into practice—through church leadership, specialized music leadership, specialized music participants, music education programs, and congregational singing.

Understanding the principles of the preceding chapters is paramount in determining the purpose of a children's choir program. And without a clear understanding of purpose we have no reason to exist.

If there is any crucial focus, it is the plea for balance—balance of all the biblical elements. We have observed the devastating effects of imbalance. The way toward balance is through a comprehensive children's choir program.

We have established our purpose scripturally. Section 2 will provide the components of educational practice. We have at our doorstep a God-given gift and a divine plan distilled throughout history. With this gift—music—through our children, we can change our culture! It has happened before. It can happen again.

1. Erik Routley, *The Church and Music.* (London: Gerald Duckworth & Co. Ltd., 1950), pp. 42-43.

2. Edwin M. Yamauchi, "The Gnostics," *The History of Christianity*, Dr. Tim Dowley, ed. (Herts, England: Lion Publishing, 1977) p. 98.

3. David F. Wright, "Councils and Creeds," *The History of Christianity*, D. Tim Dowley, ed. (Herts, England: Lion Publishing, 1977), pp. 156-157.

4. Eric Werner, *The Sacred Bridge.* (New York: Columbia University Press, 1959), p. 155.

5. Routley, *op. cit.*, p. 125.

6. Rev. David Breed, *The History and Use of Hymns and Hymn-Tunes.* (Chicago: Fleming H. Revell Co., 1903), p. 54.

7. *Ibid.*, p. 55.

8. *Ibid.*, pp. 16-18.

9. *Ibid.*, p. 21.

10. Werner, *op. cit.*, p. 211.

11. Breed., *op. cit.*, p. 17.

12. Erik Routley, *Hymns and Human Life.* (Grand Rapids: Wm. B. Eerdmans Publishing Co., 1952), p. 20.

13. *Ibid.*, p. 21.

14. Walter E. Buszin, "Luther on Music, *Musical Quarterly*, Vol. 32 (January 1946), p.83.

15. Buszin, p. 87.

16. William J. Reynolds, *A Survey of Christian Hymnody.* (New York: Holt, Rinehart and Winston, Inc., 1963), p. 70.

17. *Ibid.*, pp. 72-73.

18. *Ibid.*, p. 72.

19. *Ibid.*, p. 71.

20. Werner, *op. cit.*, p. 175.

21. *Ibid.*, p. 187.

22. Friedrich Blume, *Protestant Church Music.* (New York: W. W. Norton & Co., Inc., 1974), p. 600.

23. *Ibid.*, p. 601.

24. Appleby, David, *History of Church Music.* (Chicago: Moody Press, 1965), p. 145.

25. Reynolds, *op. cit.*, p. 83.

26. *Ibid.*, p. 90.

27. *Ibid.*, p. 93.

BIBLIOGRAPHY
for Part One

Appleby, David. P. *History of Church Music*. Chicago: Moody Press, 1965.

Bailey, Albert Edward. *The Gospel in Hymns*. New York: Charles Scribner's Sons, 1950.

Blume, Friedrich. *Protestant Church Music*. New York: W. W. Norton & Co., Inc., 1974.

Breed, David R. *The History and Use of Hymns and Hymn-Tunes*. Chicago: Fleming H. Revell Company, 1903.

Buszin, Walter E. *Cantors at the Crossroads*. St. Louis, Missouri: Concordia Publishing House, 1967.

Douglas, Winfred. *Church Music in History and Practice*. New York: Charles Scribner's Sons, 1962.

Gelineau, Rev. Joseph. (Translated by Rev. Clifford Howell). *Voices and Instruments in Christian Worship*. Collegeville, Minnesota: The Liturgical Press, 1964.

Ingram, Madeline D. *Organizing and Directing Children's Choirs*. New York: Abingdon Press, 1959.

Lovelace, A. C., and Rice, W. C. *Music and Worship in the Church*. Nashville: Abingdon Press, 1960.

McCommon, Paul. *Music in the Bible*. Nashville: Convention Press, 1956.

Northcott, Cecil. *Hymns in Christian Worship*. Richmond, Virginia: John Knox Press, 1964.

Osbeck, Kenneth W. *The Ministry of Music*. Grand Rapids, Michigan: Kregel Publications, 1961.

Parker, William H. *Psalmody of the Church*. Chicago: Hack & Anderson, Publishers, 1889.

Pierik, Marie. *The Psalter in the Temple and the Church*. Washington, D.C.: The Catholic University of America Press, 1957.

Reynolds, William Jensen. *A Survey of Christian Hymnody*. New York: Holt, Rinehart and Winston, Inc., 1963.

Rothmuller, Aron Marko. *The Music of the Jews*. South Brunswuck, New Jersey, 1967.

Routley, Erik. *Hymns and Human Life*. Grand Rapids, Michigan: Wm. B. Eerdmans Publishing Co., 1952.

Routley, Erik. *Hymns Today and Tomorrow*. New York: Abingdon Press, 1964.

Routley, Erik. *The Music of Christian Hymnody*. London: Independent Press Limited, 1957.

Sallee, James. *A History of Evangelistic Hymnody*. Grand Rapids, Michigan: Baker Book House, 1978.

Sample, Mabel Warkentin. *Leading Children's Choirs*. Nashville: Broadman Press, 1966.

Werner, Eric. *The Sacred Bridge*. New York: Columbia University Press, 1959.

Wilson, John F. *An Introduction to Church Music*. Chicago: Moody Press, 1965.

Part Two

EDUCATIONAL PERSPECTIVES

5
The Concerns of the Teacher

> The teacher is an observer, a listener, a gatherer of data, a diagnostician, a sympathetic friend, a shoulder to cry on, a suggester of ways and means to complete tasks, a dispenser of information, a staunch colleague to other teachers, a seeker of cooperative relationships with parents ... an adviser, a reminder, an evaluator, and a let-goer.
> *David A. Thatcher*

THERE ARE NO TWO WAYS about it: teaching is a tremendous task! The responsibility is compounded when children are the object of our instruction—both because children are some of the most aggressive learners and because children are in the formative stages. Everything we put in during childhood, both tangible information as well as intangible attitudes and examples, becomes incorporated into the individual and contributes to the outcome of the development process as the child matures into adulthood.

Music education for children represents a tremendous opportunity and challenge. We have examined the potential of a program founded in biblical purpose. Now the challenge is to equip individuals to fulfill this exciting ministry. What are the concerns of the teacher? What needs to be taken into consideration before he or she begins?

A basic understanding of the learning process is essential. The next four chapters examine learning from the perspective of the teacher, the student, the curriculum, and the process (or methodology). The considerations *before learning can take place* are readiness, motivation, retention, and the qualities and qualifications necessary to lead children in music—which we will examine in this chapter. The areas or domains *in which learning takes place* are cognitive, affective, and psychomotor—which are discussed in the next chapter. The materials *with which learning takes place* (at least in music) are instructional objectives, proper sequence, and evaluation—our discussion in chapter 7. And the process or *methodology for learning* music involves experiencing, learning (which encompasses many stages), and development—our topic for chapter 8.

THE CHILD'S READINESS

Public education takes great pride in synchronizing educational material with the child's development. One of the most important objectives of kindergarten and preschool teachers is to establish readiness. We have reading readiness and math readiness programs as well as countless other experiences that prepare the child for elementary academics. But what about music? When is the proper time to begin music instruction? What are the factors that establish and develop music readiness?

For many years it was thought that children should not be involved in music instruction until they were old enough to read and understand basic mathematical concepts—as well as have fairly well-developed fine motor coordination. The reasons for this were obvious. Music instruction was taxonomy-oriented—that is, you had to know what everything was and how it worked before you could perform it. In other words, you had to know what a quarter note was, how it worked, how it fit into the overall structure, and the specific letter name of the note before you could even begin to participate in music. Unfortunately, this approach resulted in a high attrition rate. More than 75 percent of the children who began music instruction at age seven or eight discontinued it by the age of nine or ten. They were involved only long enough to know that there were far too many details to learn before they could see any success.

Researchers began examining the problem and found that the critical areas had to do with understanding the child's readiness. Seven- and eight-year-old children are not ready to sit still for thirty minutes while the teacher dispenses facts about music, and then try to apply them to whatever instrument they may be learning. Children learn best by being involved in successful experiences.

The second thing they discovered was that music—like language—was primarily experienced through the ear, and 70 percent of the ear developed between the ages of three and seven. They observed that we were killing much music instruction before it even began, simply by neglecting the principles of readiness. We were, on the one hand, neglecting the years of maximum ear training and development, and on the other hand teaching with an approach that the children were not ready to handle.

For these reasons music pedagogy has undergone significant changes in the past thirty years. Current teaching techniques will be examined in chapter 8, but here we need to establish the principles of readiness.

We have seen that principal development of the ear takes place in early childhood. This fact is illustrated by the child's learning to talk. If we were to deprive children from experiencing language until they were old enough to conjugate verbs and diagram sentences, many of them would never learn to talk—at least with any facility or highly developed communication skills. Because music is an aural art, it is likewise experienced through the ear. Young children are capable of experiencing more intricate melodies and rhythms than once thought possible. A child who is exposed to a musical environment will hum the tunes he hears and sing the songs he listens to without even being prodded—it is a natural expression.

The second factor in establishing musical readiness is that of the developing voice. Children like to experiment with their voice. Many of the sounds are controlled, many are not. However, those sounds that are reinforced are repeated and developed until the child has them under control. Again, we see a tremendous correlation with the development of speech. Vocal technicians tell us that the greatest amount of vocal flexibility or malleability is prior to the age of twelve. It is after that point that vocal range begins to narrow and become more limited. While there may be a proper sequence of melodic experiences that are easiest for the child to reproduce, nevertheless we must not neglect the fact that children have a tremendous amount of vocal flexibility, and when properly developed can become successful singers at very early ages.

Another factor involved in evaluating a child's readiness is his emotional development. The way a child feels about certain experiences will ultimately have an effect on his learning. And the kind of feeling generated by the experience itself will have a determining effect on the child's attitude toward the experience. Happy music creates happy feelings. Music speaks to the emotions in communicating joy, sadness, tension, relaxation, activity, or restfulness. It also communicates from the emotions by giving the child the vehicle of expressing these same feelings—and any others he may feel at the time.

Music is also a significant factor in developing attitudes toward other things. We saw in chapter 1 that music was an important means of expressing praise, thankfulness, adoration, commitment, confession, and petition. It is essential in understanding the readiness of the child that we remember that childhood is the time when these attitudes are established. Of particular importance for the church is understanding that this kind of emotional development is an essential ingredient in their Christian education and music education programs. If we are to synchronize the development of the individual with our curriculum contents, we must include these experiences when the individual is most ready—childhood.

The final aspect to take into consideration in establishing a child's readiness for music instruction is an examination of his intellectual development. By the time a child enters the first grade he or she is ready for the activities that develop literacy. Intellectually, most children have developed to the point where they are able to comprehend certain symbols—letters or numbers—representing certain sounds or amounts. They have developed the visual discrimination necessary to recognize these symbols with repeated accuracy. And they are developing the fine motor control necessary to reproduce these symbols in their own handwriting. While all of this may not initially alter their own language experience—the way they talk—it is a necessary factor in providing for the child "tools of his own" so he can experience another person's communication through reading and likewise communicate his own experiences to others who may never hear him talk. In other words, giving the child his own set of intellectual tools is essential for continued development. Sequentially it is subsequent to his experience, but without it, illiteracy will result and deprive the student of proper development. Literacy skills are most readily established in childhood.

Elementary children are capable of the visual discrimination required to recognize specific notes on the staff, read melodic passages, and recognize specific rhythmic patterns. They are capable of writing the melodic sequences they hear or the rhythms performed if they have learned in the proper sequence. Childhood is one of the periods of most aggressive intellectual development. After the age of twelve, intellectual development definitely slows down. To deprive children of music education that involves intellectual aspects is to deny the principle of readiness. Just because music education was frequently dead-ended because of its heavy emphasis on literacy first, then experience, does not mean that music literacy is invalid. It simply means that we must change our sequence—experience first, then literacy—and alter our approach—instead of requiring children to sit still while we dispense knowledge to them, we must involve them in experiences that will have them actively participating in acquiring their desired skill. Childhood is the time of maximum readiness.

One added factor regarding the readiness of the child for music involvement is the dimension of social development. Children are developing socially. It is interesting to watch their world change from one that is dominated completely by adults—mom, dad, grandparents, etc.—to one that is preoccupied with peer relationships. Music provides for peer involvement. It is not only an individual experience, but a group activity. Groups of children can sing parts, can design and lead rhythmic activities, and can participate in text memorization. Music gives ample opportunity for the development of peer relationships. Many children who are terrorized by the aloneness of solo performance, whether musically or just giving an individual response to a question, will be easily absorbed into the ensemble experience of a music group. No longer does the responsibility for success

79

depend solely on him. It can be shared by a group. Because music involves group participation it can help children develop socially—playing and working together, so that through team effort and cooperation they can achieve something that none of them could achieve on their own.

MOTIVATION

The second area of concern for any teacher is how he or she can motivate his or her students musically. Once we are committed to a purpose and understand their readiness, how do we go about generating the kind of motivation necessary to initiate and perpetuate an exciting program? What are the factors that govern motivation? And what are some ways that we can increase motivation? Are there things that need to be avoided because they decrease motivation?

Motivation is a force. It is the energizing thrust that provides the power for the learning process. In order for this force to operate, there must be something to be achieved. In order for achievement to exist, there must be a gap—a space between where the student is, both in terms of capability and experience, and where we are offering him an opportunity to be. Because not all children are motivated by the same opportunities for achievement, a good children's music program will provide a variety of opportunities for development. Many children's choirs have trouble recruiting singers because the children do not have any concept of what it is they will achieve. Other times their achievement is only in the area of performance—we expect them to come week after week to rehearsal and then perform two or three times a year. While the knowledge of this far-off reward may be sufficient to motivate a few to trudge week after week to rehearsal, most of the children do not have the perseverance to attend rehearsals all fall for the Christmas performance. Nor is performance that important to many children.

Some churches seem to solve the problem by only having children's choir when they are preparing for a program—a sorry commentary on the total significance of a substantial music program in the life of the child. Others toil along week after week with their faithful few, and then have a tremendous influx a few weeks before the performance. This method of operation unfortunately reinforces unfaithfulness

80

and is demoralizing to those who have come faithfully throughout the year. The third alternative frequently accepted is just to assume that only a small percentage of the children within any given church will actually be interested in a music program, and therefore be content with the faithful few.

Each of these approaches neglects our first basic principle of motivation. First of all, we need to motivate by exhibiting a highly specific knowledge of areas of achievement, and because we want to involve as many children as possible, we must make our areas of achievement as varied as possible. Repertoire singing, staff reading, rhythmic participation, music relay races, contests, composition opportunities, musicals, drama, narrative parts, performances, and many other areas of development are part of any comprehensive children's music program. Not only will these varied opportunities appeal to a variety of children, but they will make the rewards more immediate. *The reward of achievement builds the person and thus will outlast the effectiveness of a small tangible prize.* If performance is the only achievement, a child must exhibit a tremendous amount of endurance before he experiences the reward. If, however, there is achievement inherent in each of the contributing activities—whether individually identifying a certain note or leading the class in a rhythm response—then the reward of achievement is experienced many times throughout the rehearsal. The end result is that force that keeps the kids coming back with excitement week after week—motivation.

The second basic criterion for motivation to be in operation is the understanding that motivation thrives in a pleasant environment. It is amazing how many churches and schools relegate music to small, dark, depressing rooms. And it is even more amazing how many children's choir directors never do anything about their rooms. Bulletin boards, wall decorations, paint, all have an effect upon the child's motivation. We cannot hope to get kids excited about participating in our music program if the room looks like it was designed for a concentration camp! The children's choir room is the home of the program. If it is fun, exciting, and worthwhile, the room will say so. If it is dull, repetitive, and monotonous the room will reflect that as well. A pleasant environment enhances the motivational process.

More important than the facility, however, is the person in charge—the director. Pleasant feelings are not only the result of an environment but are the expression of a personality. Later in this chapter we will discuss the qualities and qualifications of a good children's choir director, but we must point out here that the pleasant feelings created by the director will have a direct bearing on the motivation of the children. Directors need to organize their choirs in such a way that the children do not feel hierarchy or a caste system. They need to know that they are all important members and that their group effort results in the success of the choir. Constant rotation of leadership positions, and even structuring activities that may be group-oriented but not necessitate a "leader," tends to create pleasant feelings within the group. Acknowledging various kinds of leadership—one child may have a good voice and be a good soloist, another may have good organizational skills and help with music distribution while another may be particularly rhythmic and lead in rhythmic participation—will reinforce the worth of each individual child and create pleasant feelings, thereby increasing motivation.

Positive reinforcement enhances a pleasant environment. Many children have been lost to our children's choir programs because they have been overwhelmed with what they could not do—they couldn't carry a tune or sit still for an hour and rehearse—rather than what they could do. Children are no different than adults. None of us likes to do the things that make us look inept, clumsy, or stupid. Neither do children! The tragedy with many children's music programs is that in their attempt to be unique, they have become exclusive—excluding those children who are classified as "non-musical." Such categorization is unfair! Music has many ingredients. Just because a child does not "carry a tune" by the time he is six or seven does not mean he is not a musical child. Inability to reproduce a melody correctly can be the result of many factors—lack of exposure or experience, psychological blocks such as fear of failure, or physical immaturity. Solutions to these and other problems will be discussed later. The key factor here is to remember that underscoring a child's inability to sing a melody, reproduce a rhythm, or memorize a text will only magnify to the child what he *cannot* do—and will defeat his motivation. Finding those things that a child *can* do and magnifying those will diminish his seeming inabilities and provide motivation for him to continue developing and conquering! Many children that begin the year unable to "carry a tune" find text memorization easy, or quickly master note identification. Reinforcement in these areas while working on those that need improvement will provide motivation that will perpetuate involvement rather than discouragement that leads to dropping out.

A third factor in creating a pleasant environment is the director's attitude toward himself. A relaxed attitude and good sense of humor go a long way in creating positive feelings. Every good director needs the ability to laugh at himself, for we all make mistakes—even the most professionally trained—and sometimes at the most inopportune times. A director who responds with tension and defensiveness will engender the same kind of response in the children when they make mistakes. A carefree attitude and light-hearted chuckle will let the children know that the director is indeed human and capable of mistakes just as they are. The manner in which children handle their moments of musical frustration is frequently a reflection of the way we handle them. A tense attitude reinforces the failure and discourages motivation. A sense of humor helps the director relax, helps the children relax with themselves and their director, and stimulates motivation.

The converse of these considerations is also true. Just as motivation can be an energizing force in a positive direction, the lack of motivation or negative motivation can be a destructive force—one that will defeat not only our program but our purpose as well. What are the factors that contribute to such disaster?

Lack of recognition is one. Anonymity diminishes motivation. Just as reinforcement of individual importance is essential for group success, so the neglect of individuals into the oblivion of the group decreases individual importance, responsibility, and ultimately motivation. Nothing is more devastating to a child in a choir of seventy-five or eighty children than to have the director call on him as "you, in the last row with the green shirt behind the girl in the red dress. . . ." Many children in school regard music as less important than other subjects because the music teacher doesn't even consider it important enough to learn their names. When a director or teacher does not know individual names it is impossible for him to motivate individually, reinforce individually, and build the personal relationship that will result in providing the optimum learning experience for the child.

The absence of positive reinforcement creates discouragement and frequently fosters negative behavior patterns. Children thrive on attention and recognition just as adults do. E. L. Thorndike and B. F. Skinner established the "Law of Reinforcement," which simply states that "behavior which achieves desirable consequences will recur." These desirable consequences are most frequently, and most effectively, the verbal reinforcement of the teacher or director. When a child does not receive this assurance it not only promotes confusion—"What do I need to do to satisfy my director?"—it discourages motivation—"No matter what I do, it just isn't good enough, so I may as well not try." Communicating pleasant feelings sparks motivation. Communicating negative feelings can be a deterrent for recurring undesirable behavior. However, neutral feelings, neither complimenting them when they do well nor showing disappointment when they perform less than satisfactorily, provide a lack of motivation. To pass off something as satisfactory that was really less than satisfactory is insulting to the children. They know better.

Too much routine also nourishes a lack of motivation. When a routine becomes a rut and a teacher's techniques become too predictable, children are likely to "tune out" because of the "I know what's coming" syndrome. Children are motivated to listen when they feel that they have to listen or they might miss something important or fun or exciting. The key is to provide just enough routine so the children feel secure, but enough variety and intrigue to catch their interest.

Another cause of a motivation shortage can be a lack of personal enthusiasm on the part of the director. While it is not necessary to enter each session with a cheerleader's "rah rah" attitude, it is necessary to show that you are genuinely excited about what you're doing. Boredom on the part of the teacher creates boredom on the part of the students. Children are perceptive. They can feel when a director is acting out of obligation, or out of genuine interest and enthusiasm—both for them individually and the potential of the program as well.

Finally, lack of eye contact lessens motivation. A person's eyes have the ability to communicate a whole host of feelings—warmth, reassurance, excitement, pleasure, love, or dissatisfaction, confusion, boredom, or anger. To deny young musicians eye contact is to prevent them from getting the personal communication they deserve. One of the first things that must be taught in any music program is the necessity of watching the conductor. This goal can never be achieved if the conductor doesn't first establish eye contact with those in his choir.

Motivation, on the other hand, can be increased by active participation—whether through the use of visual aids such as an overhead projector, chalkboard, or specifically designed student materials, or by using rhythm instruments or body involvement—body percussions, choreography, or creative responses. Motivation is increased when there is a relationship between music and other areas of interest to the child. Many times a hymn has an interesting story behind how it was written, or it was composed at a time in history when certain other events might provide interest for the child, or maybe the children have been working on a certain rhythmic or melodic sequence and it is incorporated into a song. Whatever the situation, we need to constantly establish these relationships to other experiences of interest.

When our programs suffer from lack of interest we need to take a careful perceptive look at our program and personnel. Is there achievement inherent in our program? Is it the kind of achievement that encompasses a variety of areas, not just performance? Is accomplishment evidenced in every rehearsal in many different aspects so that the rewards of success are experienced frequently? What about the environment? Is it conducive to learning, or does it diminish motivation? And what about personal leadership? Is it characterized by positive reinforcement, personal warmth, and pleasant attitudes?

85

We must remember that the art of motivation is found in structuring a program of moderate difficulty—easy enough to be achievable with work, but difficult enough so that when we succeed we feel some satisfaction. Achievement and the reward of success need to be constantly experienced by the children. Pleasant feelings and personal enthusiasm create the environment for motivation to flourish. A major concern of the teacher—one that must always be at the forefront of his or her awareness, one that will ultimately determine the success of the entire children's music program—must be motivation.

RETENTION

The third area of concern for the children's music director is the matter of retention—not just the kind of retention that will get our children successfully through their performances without forgetting song texts and spoken lines, but the kind of retention that will provide substantial building blocks in establishing a program of individual and group significance. Very few directors would consider a children's music program worth their effort if they thought that six months or a year later the children would forget everything they had learned. Very few would dedicate themselves to preparation and rehearsal week after week if they felt in the long run that what they were doing would not substantially matter in the children's lives.

How does retention happen? Just because children are able to learn quickly and easily, does that in itself insure that they will remember what we teach them? Does good intention and faithful attendance insure substantial building blocks—the kind that will have a determining influence in the life of the individual child? How can we know, in the long run, what has been remembered and what has provided a foundation for future development?

We have already alluded to the three areas of the personality involved in the learning process—the intellect, the feelings, and the physical experience. These areas of learning are the same for child and adult. We will be examining them more closely in the next chapter. However, we must make preliminary observations here because they are not only concerns of the student, but of the teacher as well, and especially as they relate to the matter of retention. Why? Because retention is directly proportional to the involvement of the student in these three learning domains.

We have noted that the predominant approach to children's music education for many years has been to bog them down with multitudinous details prior to their experiencing any fulfilling music participation. We observed how this has been counter-productive in terms of continuing music education and musical motivation. The other fallacy of this approach is that it places much emphasis on cognitive learning (i.e. memorizing a long list of musical facts—the names of the lines and spaces, kinds of notes, definition of terms such as "time signature" and "key signature"). As a result, it denies equal participation for the other areas involved in the learning apparatus—the affective domain, which is the subjective dimension of the personality; and the psychomotor domain, which deals with physical experience. In so doing, retention is severely curtailed. It is pointless to memorize the names of the lines and spaces using such gimmicks as "Every Good Boy Does Fine" unless we are prepared to tie it to the musical experience of the child. There simply is no need to know the names of notes until you are ready to use them—either by playing an instrument, singing them, recognizing a melodic passage, writing a melodic pattern, or any other creative usage.

Teachers who spend lesson after lesson on such musical facts without giving students opportunity to use them can be sure of one thing—a very short retention rate. This is why so many children remember "nothing" a few months afterward. While it is fair to assume that retention will diminish without constant usage, it is equally realistic to assume that if a child has been involved in meaningful learning, a major portion of the material will remain with him for an extensive amount of time. The problem comes when we assume just because a child is able to recite a list of memorized musical facts that he has learned them. Hardly. Cognitive learning is only one area of the total learning apparatus of the individual. Thirty-three percent cannot be considered a passing grade.

On the other hand, there are approaches to children's music education that in an attempt to reverse the problem we have just described, have eliminated all cognitive aspects of learning and dealt only with the experience—psychomotor. This methodology involves the children in one musical experience after another without ever tying them to the musical facts. This technique usually, although not always, takes the form of rote instruction with the teacher providing the information—melody, rhythm, or text—and the student copying what he or she has heard. This approach also has severe limitations in terms of retention. Why? Because the experince aspect is also only *one* of the areas involved in the learning process. And when experience is not tied to cognitive and affective learning, retention is likewise diminished. Also, when the learning process depends entirely on the teacher being the information dispensary, we keep the student from developing tools of his own, which inevitably provide the building blocks for future musical development. In order for retention to be significant, we must involve *all* areas of the learning apparatus.

In order for quarter notes to be meaningful they need to be experienced—perhaps with a hand clap or finger snap. They need to be visualized—the child needs to see what it is he has been experiencing. Then children need to combine their experience and visualization—perhaps clap the rhythmic pattern while reading it from the chalkboard, or overhead projector. That experience can then be expanded upon—perhaps by altering it slightly or adding vocal or instrumental participation. Finally, it can be written down, which ties the knot in the learning process. Writing takes the information from the abstract—the *teacher's* quarter notes on the chalkboard—and makes them the personal property of the child. Now they are *his* quarter notes because he wrote them. When a child has experienced quarter notes, visualized quarter notes, combined his experience with visualization, expanded his usage, and written them, we do not have to worry whether or not he will remember them—they are his forever!

The same sequence holds true for staff reading and melodic recognition. Patterns can be sung, visualized, then sightsung, varied and expanded, and finally written to insure mastery and retention. Texts from songs and Scriptures can be recited, combined with physical or rhythmic participation, sequenced through word games, expanded to daily experiences, and restated through creative composition. Specific techniques, obviously, should vary from one song to another and one rehearsal to another; the expectation of retention demands comprehensive learning—structuring curriculum to involve every aspect of the personality.

One of the reasons that comprehensive learning has frequently been ignored is that comprehensive retention has seldom been evaluated. In too many cases, the only retention evaluation we have is performance and repertoire—we consider ourselves successful if the children remember their words and their parts for the performance. While this may exhibit immediate retention, it cannot be expected to measure long-range retention any more than memorizing the dates of the Civil War battles for a U.S. History test measured the overall importance of our secondary education. If we expect substantial ingredients to be remembered and built upon, then we must extract those key items and apply them to more than one isolated song or musical experience. These items need to become the building blocks that can apply wholeness to our purpose, and must be infused into every element of our program. Long-range goals and retention are inseparable partners.

A biblically based children's music program will have specific long-range goals in terms of biblical education (as described in the first four chapters of this book), music education (including all elements of music literacy, appreciation, and involvement), and opportunities for ministry (everything from our church concerts to outreach possibilities). Once these goals are established, we can view those essential ingredients that will contribute to the overall purpose of our program with accurate perspective rather than the frequent "near-sightedness" that sees only as far as the next performance.

We examined the role that pleasant feelings play in establishing musical motivation. They also play a significant role in retention. Giving children the opportunity to express verbally or in other creative ways—compositionally or artistically—grants them the opportunity to respond personally to the musical experience. One of the benefits of classroom or group music instruction is that it provides for corporate and individual involvement at the same time. However, if retention is to be achieved, we must allow individuals to express back in some way what they have learned. In so doing, we again take the corporate experience and translate it into individualized learning. It is equally important that this individual response not be a carbon copy of the teacher's musical instruction, but allows for the creativity of the individual. This allowance encourages the individual child to take the musical experience and make it his own.

Taking a fundamental truth of Scripture such as Creation, or praise or thanksgiving, memorizing a Scripture, but then allowing the child to express the meaning of the verse as it relates to him individually, will increase his retention because he has personalized the information. Relating the text of a song to an incident in history or an event that took place in the Bible, or a situation that a child encounters will inevitably increase his retention. Letting him select an opening or closing measure from a list of appropriate selections will allow the child to take his factual knowledge and add to it the personal touch of melodic and rhythmic expression. Individual responses are essential ingredients in retention.

After we have involved all areas of the learning apparatus, selected key ingredients, and allowed for individual response, we have the next area that is essential if retention is to occur. Positive transfer is the result of information that has been thoroughly learned to the extent that the same information or musical facts can be rearranged or used in a different situation with equal accuracy. One simple example of positive transfer is to lead the children in clapping the simple rhythm ♩♩♩♪ . Then you may have them snap it or do it with another body percussion. You might choose to add a musical accompaniment—such as record or piano. Once the experience is successful, you can show the children what they were performing by drawing ♩♩♩♪ on the chalkboard, overhead projector, or showing it to them on a flashcard. Then the children should experience it along with the visualization. You can expand their learning experience by having them perform it on a rhythm instrument. Then have them write it for themselves and clap their own for the class. Because they have learned the name "quarter note" and "quarter rest" you are preparing them for positive transfer because you have extracted the vital information instead of just leaving it as a one-time-only cute musical game. Then you can show the class ♩♪♩♪ and ask for a volunteer to clap what they think it will sound like—because they *know* all the vital information necessary to perform the rhythm. All that is required is positive transfer—the ability to take the same information, knowing what quarter notes and quarter rests are, and apply it in another situation.

One of the reasons much long-range retention is lost in our children's music programs is that too many times the musical information we give the child is limited to only one place or time. This prevents positive transfer. One of the reasons that "every good boy does fine" has produced so many people who can read the treble clef and not the bass clef is that it cannot be transferred. It is information that is only correct in one isolated instance. Rather, if we would teach the musical alphabet as being A-B-C-D-E-F-G—which is always correct regardless of clef, the information could be equally transferred to bass, alto, or tenor clef with accuracy.

The same concept holds true in evaluating the significant retention in children's choir programs that merely proceed from one musical to the next. Because the entire children's music program is outlined in performance, it many times fails to give the child essential ingredients that can be transferred into his overall development. All that is left when they graduate from our children's choir is the nice memory of some musical performances with little that can be transferred into later life. How much more meaningful it would be to provide a comprehensive program—one that would provide the individual with the significant building blocks that will continue to have an effect and allow for future development in later years. Retention requires positive transfer.

Finally, retention demands practice and reinforcement. It is important to note the choice of words here—*practice* and *reinforcement,* not *repetition* or *redundancy.* Too many times in our attempt for retention we treat our children like a drill team—going over and over and over again, until we assume that they MUST get it—if not by their own brilliance then by our persistence. Unfortunately, while repetition may aid in retention up to a certain point, after that certain point,

91

it can actually diminish retention, or prove counter-productive. More effective than protracted exact repetition is the concept of practice—mastering the same material, whether rhythmic pattern, melodic sequence, or song text, in a variety of ways. Many masterful musicians in teaching their students an instrumental solo will have them practice it a variety of ways—sometimes very slow, other times very fast, sometimes beginning in the middle. Why? All are techniques to vary the practice because retention is increased more by "practice" than "repetition."

Reinforcement is that personal encouragement given by the director-teacher. Just as it is significant in motivation, it influences retention. Reinforcement is the openness to creative stimulus that good teaching fosters. It is the constant looking for new ways to express old ideas and previously learned information. It provides for the child the "I can do it" confidence that encourages experimentation and further development. Once these forces are at work, retention comes naturally.

PERSONAL QUALIFICATIONS AND QUALITIES

So far we have only examined the concerns of the teacher in relationship to the children. Our examination would be incomplete without also looking at the concerns of the teacher in relationship to his or her own personal preparation. Many times we become so overwhelmed with the need of the students (or the program) that we forget to scrutinize our own capacity to adequately fill the need.

Good children's music directors are a beautiful blend of qualifications and qualities. Sometimes excellent candidates exclude themselves from vital ministry under the guise of not being as qualified as they ought to be, or not as qualified as someone else in the congregation. Conversely, many times we designate leadership based on a long list of credentials and fail to take into consideration that it is not credentials alone that make a good teacher. It is the blending of the two that provides capable leadership in our children's music programs.

What should be our minimal guidelines in selecting competent children's musical leadership in the church or Christian school? Although many schools do not face the problem of evaluating musical qualifications—that has been done for them by a credentialing board or college education—still they need to discern with great perception those qualities that cannot be measured by testing, credentials or classroom work.

Music literacy is a prerequisite for teaching music and directing children's choirs. This is usually not a problem in the schools, but is frequently a problem in the local church. We have noted the absolute necessity of providing the children with musical "tools" of their own if our music program is to develop continued musical initiative. It is impossible to teach children to read music if we do not read it ourselves. While it may not be necessary to decipher a symphonic score in order to lead a children's choir, it is equally naive to assume that a person who considers himself "musical" but doesn't read music can teach music to children. Music literacy includes melodic and rhythmic accuracy. One must know note names and be able to accurately read rhythms.

There are some directors who do not consider themselves proficient at staff reading, but because they understand the importance of this ingredient, take it upon themselves to learn to read music. Sometimes they may be only a step or two ahead of the children, but in each case, the awareness of the need and constant pursuit of music literacy skills help overcome this deficiency. While this may not always be the best situation, it can be successful if a person is willing to work on this area of need. None of us, no matter how qualified, should ever be willing to teach only out of our knowledge—we should always be learning and acquiring new skills.

In addition to music literacy, a certain amount of music facility needs to be exhibited. Not every good director needs to play the piano, but if he doesn't, he certainly needs the assistance of a good accompanist. If not proficient on an instrument, however, directors need to display their musical ability some other way—preferably in vocal facility. Because children learn by imitation as well as instruction, it is difficult to teach children to sing if the director isn't an adequate singer. This does not mean that every children's choir director needs to be a polished soloist, but the director must be able to carry a tune accurately, produce a pleasant tone, and understand enough about good vocal production to illustrate it and develop it in the children.

Third, a basic knowledge of <u>simple conducting techniques</u> is most helpful. The physical contortions that many directors go through in trying to communicate to their choirs is amazing. Many justify this with a "well, it works" mentality, failing to see that adequate training involves providing musical direction that can be transferred to other directors in other situations. Yes, conducting style is a personalized technique, but there are basic standards that all should incorporate into their directing. This not only provides good training for the children, but certainly facilitates the use of accompaniment instruments—whether keyboard, small ensemble, or complete symphony.

The following diagrams depict the basic conducting patterns:

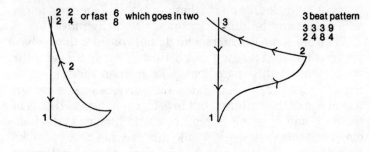

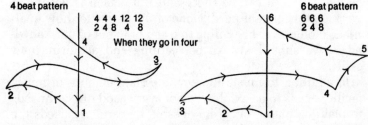

An appreciation for a wide <u>variety of musical styles</u> will help a director provide a well-balanced music program. In the first section of this book we examined the three biblical archetypes and discussed the importance of each. A children's music director must provide all three types of music for the corporate and individual well-being of the choir.

Therefore, he must be able to interpret different musical styles accurately. Dynamics, tempo, phrasing, nuances, and all interpretive techniques need to be appropriate for the type of music sung.

One of the most helpful ways to improve one's directing skills is to observe good directors. Take time to attend other children's programs, music classes, and choir rehearsals. Observe what techniques enhance the success of other music directors. Learn what approaches to avoid. Try to improve your effectiveness by learning from others who have differing strengths from your own.

One factor often overlooked in evaluating qualifications is the alignment of purpose. Musical and educational criteria alone are inadequate in deciding if a certain person can fill a certain job. In order for a children's music director to operate a successful program, he or she needs to be certain that the specific goals and purpose that he has set for the program align with the goals and purpose of administrative superiors—whether that be the music minister, senior minister, Christian school principal, or governing board. Nonalignment of purpose can be most frustrating for a children's music program, the director of the program, and administrative personnel. Alignment of purpose will incorporate educational, musical, and ministry objectives with the overall program of the local church or school. It will need to take into consideration not only group benefits but individual benefits as well, for when mass programming purposes are pursued at the expense of individual worth, our programs become another assembly line for rubber stamp Christians who are incapable of incorporating fundamental truth into their daily life situations.

But qualifications are only one side of the coin. Qualifications, even a prestigious pedigree, cannot in themselves insure a good children's music director. Because we are working with people—precious children—who respond as persons and not as robots, knowing how to relate is as important as knowing music.

Loving and learning go hand in hand. It is more important for teachers to love what they are doing than to have an extended list of what they know. It is not sufficient for directors just to love directing or teaching per se, but they must have a love for the children—as a group, and a love for each child. How a child feels about being in our music program is just as important as anything we can teach him.

Love for the children will foster the building of relationships—the kind that will go beyond our music rehearsals into other areas of the child's world. Life is lived in the arena of relationships. Any program that seeks significance in personal growth and development must understand that loving and learning are inseparable.

Tact has become almost a lost art in today's educational circles. With the emphasis on communicating what a person really feels, we have discarded tact along with the facades and pretense of Victorianism that denied truthfulness for social acceptability. But tact is not pretense. Tact is a combination of sensitivity and perceptivity that controls the manner with which we communicate, not the content. The tactful person understands that while he may have to express something unpleasant in content, it can be communicated without undue hurt.

Good children's workers must exhibit tact. Many times it will be necessary to enforce discipline or policy, communicate with nonsympathetic parents, assign soloists, audition for special ensembles or parts, and make other difficult decisions. Without tact, these responsibilities can be hurtful, embarrassing, and threatening. With tact, there pervades a mutual respect and tolerance. It is the demonstration of "speaking the truth in love." A good children's director will be sensitive to the needs of the children and will endeavor to look at things through the child's perspective. Perception means that we see through the eyes of the child.

Another essential quality for the effective children's teacher is to be genuine. This means a teacher can relate to the children on their level without talking "down" to them. It is easy for musicians to become so engrossed in their adult musical world that children are approached with a condescending attitude. Resistance and resentment are the only results. Communicating horizontally with children does not mean we must become childish. Many attempt to work with children by becoming "cutesy." Nothing is more phony to the children. They know the director is an adult and expect him to act like one.

96

The last quality we will examine here is seldom mentioned in textbooks or classes in music education. An inherent quality in a good teacher is that he or she is always open to new ideas. Nothing is quite so tragic as a person unwilling to learn—either from the children, colleagues, or superiors. Many well-intended children's music programs have fallen prey to an inflexible "expert" who had been teaching a certain way for twenty years and wasn't about to learn anything new from a "novice" in the field. Good teachers and directors are good learners—and they are constantly learning. Our children should be a constant creative stimulus—giving us new ideas, approaches, techniques, and challenges. Our colleagues are able to view our strengths and weaknesses objectively and provide input to help keep us on course rather than plowing ahead until we reach a dead end. Our superiors in the field can provide for us models of how to improve our skills and develop our ministries. Each relationship will help our ministry develop in different ways. Good directors will gladly receive input from all three. When we no longer open ourselves up for new ideas, different techniques, and creative stimulus, we will stagnate and our effectiveness will rapidly diminish. Openness to new ideas is one of the most vital qualities for anyone called to this significant ministry.

SUMMARY

Directing a children's music ministry is an exciting challenge, and much of the responsibility for its success lies in its leadership. A competent director will take into consideration three basic concerns—readiness, motivation, and retention. A qualified director will exhibit music literacy, music facility, and musical integrity. A quality teacher will demonstrate love, alignment of purpose, tact, genuineness, and a consistent openness to new ideas.

This kind of personal profile is not an illusive dream. The old adage that anything worth having is worth working for, can suitably be applied here. Anyone truly desiring a position of children's musical leadership can work diligently to acquire skills and develop qualities necessary for the job. Many times we pass off children's music leadership to unqualified people because we think it doesn't matter—"They're just children." This tragic misconception is in direct opposition to biblical principles and educational evidence.

Once we are aware of the tremendous potential of children—which all too frequently has been underestimated—we have every reason to sharpen our skills, develop personality traits, and focus our ministry into one of the most exciting opportunities in the Christian community! Too many times we have addressed only the needs of the children without taking into consideration the needs of the teacher. The needs of the teacher are as germane to the educational process as the needs of the children. The directors are the ones who touch the children's lives and interact with them. "They are the ones who implement educational (and musical) policy and curriculum content, scope and sequence; and—most important—they are the ones who establish the educational (and spiritual) climate and who structure the learning experiences."[1] A children's music director has an incredible challenge, an exciting opportunity, and a fulfilling reward.

1. David A. Thatcher, *Teaching, Loving, and Self-directed Learning.* (Pacific Palisades, California: Goodyear Publishing Company, Inc., 1973), p. 166.

6
The Needs
of the Student

There are two critical conditions of learning; characteristics of
the learner and characteristics of the situation in which learning
occurs.

A definition of learning referring to knowledge acquisition only
would be of narrow scope while one referring to the acquisition
of knowledge, attitudes, and skills would be of broad scope.[1]
Gary S. Belkin and Jerry L. Gray

EDUCATION IS A COMPLEX PROCESS. It is complex because of
personnel. It requires a teacher—and no two teachers or
directors are exactly alike. It requires students—and no two
students are exactly alike. It is complex because of situation.
No two churches or schools are exactly alike. And it is complex by definition. One person's definition of learning frequently differs considerably from another's.

Given this complex set of circumstances how is it possible
to responsibly address the area of music education for children within the Christian context—either church or school?
Our purpose is not to present a treatise on educational psychology and learning theories. Substantial research has been
done in each of these areas, and what is presented here is
based on those findings. However, for those interested in
more verification in terms of scholarly data, the bibliography
provided at the end of this section will serve as a good start.

Our purpose here is to provide a basic foundation for children's music ministry that is solidly based on biblical principles and sound educational practice.

What must we know about children to succeed in a comprehensive music program? Is it reasonable to assume that we can possibly offer a program of significance to many children, or must we satisfy ourselves with just meeting the needs of an elite few? What are the areas inherent in the learning process, and how can we know that we are effectively meeting them? At least three areas of development must be dealt with. Let's look at them one at a time.

COGNITIVE DEVELOPMENT

Cognitive development is concerned with the thinking process, with intellectual growth. It is objective in nature and is frequently measured by educators through testing.

Scripture is concerned with cognitive development. In Matthew 22:37 Jesus commands us to love God "with all your heart, and with all your soul, and with all your mind." Romans 12:2 instructs us, "And do not be conformed to this world, but be transformed by the renewing of your mind." Spiritual maturation requires intellectual development. A children's music program within the Christian context must be equally concerned with the development of cognitive skills—scriptural and musical.

Much work has been done by developmental psychologists to determine how cognitive development occurs. At the forefront has been a Swiss psychologist, Jean Piaget. One of his most significant contributions to all who work with children is the classifications of various stages of cognitive development. While we will not examine each stage, we should at least note the third stage, since that includes most elementary age children.

Beginning somewhere around the age of seven and continuing on until approximately eleven, children develop the ability to perform intellectual operations, Piaget found. Skills such as classifying information, reversing sequences, and logically explaining reasons for conclusions are all examples of this stage. Prior to this stage is the period of preoperational thought, which is characterized by learning through perception. Rather than reasoning out something logically, preoperational children draw conclusions on what they perceive through observation. Those working with children ages three to seven need to examine this stage closely.

100

Beginning somewhere in the late sixth grade, children begin to move into the next stage of development—that of formal operations—which is characterized by their ability to work with hypothetical reasoning and symbolic and abstract functions.

How does all this relate to children's music ministry? In broad terms, simply this: If our program is going to be meaningful to the children, it must be geared to the child's level of development. In specific terms, the texts of the songs in our children's repertoire must be appropriate. Many songs that have been traditionally characterized as "children's songs" or "adult songs" have suffered terrible injustice because of negligence of this principle.

Elementary age children are capable of thinking intelligently as long as the information is on the concrete level—i.e., it does not require them to operate in the abstract either in terms of understanding imagery or symbolism. Two important conclusions need to be applied to our selection of appropriate children's repertoire. First, it should say something important, and second, it should be literally true. Music that says nothing meaningful is insulting to the intelligence of a grade school child. And music that requires the understanding of imagery contributes nothing to their learning—not because of our explanation, but because of their development.

For too many years our children's music repertoire in the church has been filled with meaningless jingles that say nothing important or substantial for the child to know. We have placed so much emphasis on a child's song being "cute" that we have forgotten that children are intelligent, and songs that make little or no sense only teach him one thing: that church music is nonsense.

On the other hand, we have become so engrossed with many of the beautiful images in Scripture—Jesus as the Lamb of God, Jesus as the Rose of Sharon, God as a strong tower—that we have forgotten that children think literally and not in images. Music that refers to cups running over, bubbles inside, and shooting artillery in spiritual warfare have no comprehension on the childhood level.

Music can contribute to cognitive development if we select our texts carefully. The basic doctrines of Scripture can be learned easily by the elementary child through the selection of substantial music. Let us examine some fundamental doctrines and corresponding song texts that help the singer—whether child or adult—express this acquisition of knowledge.

Basic Doctrine	Appropriate Music Selection
Creation	"All Things Bright and Beautiful"
	"This Is My Father's World"
	"For the Beauty of the Earth"
The Church	"In Christ There is No East or West"
	"They'll Know We Are Christians"
The Character of God	"Great Is Thy Faithfulness"
	"O Mighty God, How Great Thou Art"
The Resurrection	"We Welcome Glad Easter"
	"O Sons And Daughters Let Us Sing"
The Bible	"Holy Bible, Book Divine"

The list could go on. This type of analysis lets us examine text in the light of these two critical areas: significance and imagery. Please note that the preceding suggestions are literally true. They do not require the children to move from imagery to reality for comprehension. They help the child articulate important scriptural truths.

Another area of cognitive development that is greatly increased through music is Scripture memorization. Many children memorize with ease (apparently the ability to memorize reaches its peak about the age of 7), while a few may work and work and find it impossible. Does this mean that a few children have to experience failure while others have the joy of success, or that we should eliminate much Scripture memorization from our childhood training? Experience has proven that it is easier to memorize through music, thus aiding Scripture memorization. This does not only include Scripture choruses but non-melodic, rhythmic, Scripture chants. In fact, not only does music facilitate memorization for children with average learning skills, but it also places it within the mastery range of many children with learning difficulties. Hyperactive children and youngsters with learning disabilities are frequently helped through the rhythmic speaking and body percussion techniques.

Children as young as three and four can participate in clapping and saying Genesis 1:31:

AND GOD SAW EV-'RY. - THING THAT HE HAD MADE, AND BE- HOLD IT WAS VER-Y GOOD!

It can be amplified by use of other body percussions such as the finger snap, patchen (thigh slapping), or foot stomp. It can be expressed on rhythm instruments. It can then be identified by ear—when the children hear just the rhythm and respond by repeating the verse.

Primary and junior children can learn the scriptural description of the Lord Jesus from Isaiah 9:6:

FOR UN-TO US A CHILD IS BORN. UN-TO US A SON IS GIV - EN. AND THE

GO-VERN-MENT SHALL BE UP - ON HIS SHOUL-DER. AND HIS NAME SHALL BE

CALLED WON-DER-FUL, COUN-SEL-LOR, THE MIGHT-Y GOD, THE EV-ER - LAST-ING

FA-THER, THE PRINCE OF PEACE. I- SA-IAH 9: 6

Scriptures that are sung will be remembered much longer than those that are merely recited without some corresponding body involvement—whether singing or rhythmic participation.

Piaget's findings also have clear implications regarding the relationship of music literacy skills to cognitive development. Learning to read music aids in perceptual development, spatial relationships, and reading from left to right. Music literacy increases math concepts—units, fractions, unity, and variety. Take, for instance, the following four-measure pattern.

Children can designate individual measures (complete units), individual beats (parts or fractions of the measure), unity (similarities between measures in that they each have four beats and utilize quarter notes and quarter rests), and variety (in spite of certain similarities, there are certain differences).

Staff reading encourages cognitive development. The following melody pattern helps develop spatial relationships—the equal distance between the notes in the first measure and the greater space between the notes of the second measure. It will also help him *think* which way the sound will go, whether performed vocally or instrumentally. Will it go up or down, or stay the same? By thinking and perception, combined with logic, the child can see the notes in the first measure going up and figure that the sound will also go up, and since the notes in the second measure go down, so will the sound.

Not only does music literacy contribute to cognitive development, but the potential for music literacy is greatly enhanced because of the nature of the child's development. Just as it is easier to teach children to read and write than it is to teach adults the same skills, so it is easier to teach children to develop fundamental musical skills. This fact is not a commentary on the mental capability of the individual, but rather on his or her development. Because children in the concrete operational stage are in the process of developing perceptual skills, and operating in terms of literal logic, the activities associated with becoming musically literate are more apt to be interesting to this age child. These activities coincide beautifully with all other aspects of their development.

Music is significant in its contribution to cognitive skills—both from the educational and spiritual viewpoint. The internalization of basic doctrine, the memorization of Scripture, the building of biblical vocabulary, the development of reading and math skills are only a few of the benefits afforded those who will accurately understand this capacity and need in the child's learning.

104

AFFECTIVE DEVELOPMENT

"Affective learning includes emotional learning, value learning, and character development, along with aesthetic appreciation. Through affective education, the raw materials of the emotions are translated into feelings, attitudes, and values."[1] There have been philosophers and psychologists who from ancient history have argued that cognitive learning without affective learning is not only pointless but dangerous. Plato postulated that without the operation of proper values, cognitive learning could be a destructive force because it was operating in the hands of evil men. Others point out that learning that does not affect the development of a person's character is worthless.

The time has come for the Christian community to realize that cognitive development alone is not adequate Christian education. For years we have preoccupied ourselves with memorizing assorted Bible facts—persons, places, and events, and theological minutia. All of this is worthless in terms of personal significance until we are able to translate that knowledge into character development—helping people to grow up into the person of Jesus Christ—a maturation that is evidenced by attitudes and values.

Christian maturity necessitates emotional development. Emotional health has been overlooked for years by the church as an integral part of its educational responsibility. Today's children find themselves in a state of emotional chaos. Many parents, unable to cope with economic pressures and role changes, are providing less and less emotional care and security for their young children. The breakdown of family units leaves children in a state of emotional bewilderment. And from every angle, the values traditionally held as "Christian" are being attacked. The entire value system of culture seems to be dying.

What can a children's music program do to help the situation? Music can play an important role in the character, value, and attitude development of our children. Many theologians and philosophers have done extensive research into the relationship between values in a culture and its music. Each person's research is handled in various methods and with varying presentations, but one unanimously recognizable fact is that the music of a culture and the values of a

105

culture are very closely linked. Why? Because music, as is any art, is a statement of feeling. It is the concrete expression of an attitude, feeling, or thought. By embodying this abstract concept in a concrete musical expression, we give ourselves and others who participate in its expression the opportunity to contemplate and understand the feeling that precipitated the expression in the first place. Music is more than an assortment of notes and lyrics. It is a communication.

> Participative experiences of works of art are communions—experiences so full and final that they enrich our entire lives. Such experiences are life-enhancing not just because of the great satisfaction they may give us at the moment but also because they make more or less permanent contributions to that part of our life which is yet to be.[2]

Music is not only significant in cognitive education, it is critical in affective education. Through participation in music, not only are the attitudes of the song reflected, but the attitudes, feelings, and emotions of the participants are altered.

Music has the ability to reflect as well as determine the values of a society. The music of a culture reflects its values, and thereby helps determine the values of the next generation. The dope culture, the "New Morality" and the anti-establishment philosophies of the '60's were all reflected in music. The despair and hopelessness of the same decade were poignantly expressed in Peggy Lee's song, "Is That All There Is?" Yes, music is a statement of values, attitudes, feelings, and emotions.

One of the greatest challenges of a good children's music program is to provide for the development of biblical attitudes and values, and help the children develop feelings and emotions that will produce spiritual health. This is accomplished by giving them music that reflects such biblical attitudes as love, joy, peace, patience, gentleness, goodness, faith, kindness, and temperance. These are the fruit of the Spirit—the exhibits of affective learning. This kind of development is not obtained by mere cognition—factual accumulation. It does not happen until these characteristics are observed, identified, and integrated into the fabric of the individual personality. This is affective education! And because music is an expression of feelings it is significant in the development of feelings. "Thus, arts education can be seen as not merely a luxury to be offered to only the fortunate few, but as a necessity for effective living."[3]

What are the essential affective ingredients that need to govern our children's music education programs? The first biblical value we need to reflect for our children is love, because without it, all others are unattainable. It is the foundation on which all affective or emotional development is based. We have the responsibility to reflect God's love to the children. God's love is unconditional—it is not based on physical attractiveness or expensive wardrobe. It is personal—not a corporate concern that looks upon all children as a mass, but as a composite of special individuals, each one a unique creation of a beautiful God. It will be communicated by eye contact, physical contact, focused attention, and positive discipline. It will be demonstrated by the director and the attitude he or she exhibits toward the children. But it will also be sung about. It will be amplified by Scripture memorization. Thus, the loving atmosphere the children experience from week to week will be translated into affective learning—experiencing love, feeling loved, and knowing the truths of God's love. A child that has not experienced love, does not feel loved, and will be unable to express love to God or anyone else. Conversely, those children who, through our music programs, experience love, will feel loved. They, in turn, will grow up knowing they are loved by an infinitely personal God and will be able to share his love with others.

Songs like "I'm Something Special" and "I Am a Promise" by Bill and Gloria Gaither, and the traditional "Praise Him, Praise Him, All Ye Little Children" begin to teach God's personal, unconditional love. "Jesus Loves Me, This I Know, for the Bible Tells Me So" is one of the most profound texts ever written. The recent "Oh How He Loves You and Me" by Kurt Kaiser transcends any age barrier; our need to know of God's love is not something that we outgrow after childhood. This music speaks to the child's need of self-esteem—an affective consideration, without which our cognitive input is substantially diminished.

A second attitude our children need to develop is grateful-ness. They need to be thankful for who they are. They need to develop an appreciation for others and their uniqueness, and most of all, they need an attitude of thankfulness and praise to God. Patterns of incessant complaining and severe criticism of others are established in childhood. We have the opportunity to reverse this process through our music pro-grams. Again, we establish this by first providing an atmo-sphere where each child feels genuinely appreciated. Direc-tors need to express gratitude to the children corporately and individually for cooperation, an act of helpfulness, a demon-stration of kindness or courtesy. But then we need to teach the children to be thankful. We should have them express thanks to their peers and leaders. And most importantly, we should teach them to express thanksgiving to God.

The Thanksgiving season provides a natural time to address this area of development. Scripture memorization could be Psalm 107:1:

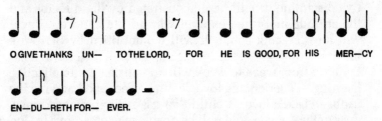

Repertoire to reinforce this truth and give the children the opportunity for personal expressions of thankfulness might be "Jesus, We Just Want to Thank You," "Thank You for Doing It So Well," "Now Thank We All Our God," and "With Thankful Hearts, O Lord, We Come."

A good project might be to list every item named in the songs as things to be thankful for—sunrise, afternoons, daily food, health, etc., and assign two or three to each child and have them make a creative musical expression of thankful-ness at home. They may want to compose a rhyme, paint a picture of the song lyrics, or create a rhythmic expression to be performed by using a body percussion or rhythm instru-ment. Then at the following rehearsal, have them share their creative expression with the class. You could follow this up by rotating the list of items for the second week. Depending on the musical facility of the group, they may be able to even compose a simple tune.

I am thank-ful   for the sun,   and strong legs that   let‑ me run.

This kind of a musical experience will have much more long-term significance in the life of the child than merely learning a Thanksgiving anthem and performing it in a service. Patterns of thankfulness will have been experienced and then translated into instruction—Scripture instruction, repertoire instruction, and opportunity for creative expression through the use of music fundamentals. This is affective development!

One final reason that makes the presence of a children's musical program even more critical in our churches and Christian schools is that *music speaks to and from the emotions.* Many times children do not need any more cognitive input or intellectual lectures. They need something that will speak directly to their emotions. Music has that capacity. It can create relaxation or tension, it can communicate cheer or sorrow, or provide soothing for emotional turmoil. Every area of society recognizes this fact. Many preschools and kindergartens play certain types of music at rest time. Grocery stores and department stores play certain kinds of music. Restaurants feature certain kinds of music in accordance with the kind of mood they want to create. Why? Because music speaks to the emotions. Feelings are created by the presence of certain types of music.

Children will inevitably come into our churches, music programs, and rehearsals with feelings of insecurity, frustration, and disappointment—maybe over the events of the day, the week, or situations at home that have caused deep emotional hurts. It is at times like this that giving them a song will do much more for them than giving them a lecture or story. The song will ring over and over in their ears long after the rehearsal is completed. The message will be internalized as the child contemplates the song in his quiet moments. Imagine the child who constantly feels he is the object of everyone's anger—"Mom and Dad are always upset at me; my teacher is always mad at me; even my friends are always beating up on me." Place into the experience of this young-ster the expression:

God is so good; God is so good;
God is so good; He's so good to me.

Not only is the child involved in an expression of the nature of God, but he is participating in an expression that takes God's goodness out of the abstract and into the personal—God is good to me! Yes, music speaks to the emotions, and helps translate them into attitudes and values.

Music also provides the child with the opportunity to speak from the emotions. One of the greatest causes of emo-tional problems is suppressed feelings. Children who have participated in musical expression have become comfortable with expressing feelings in this idiom—first the feelings of others, and then their own. While it is not safe to assume that any child who participates in music will be automatically free from emotional problems, it is safe to assume that music has become a valuable instrument in helping children who have difficulty expressing themselves begin to participate in the expression of feelings. The entire field of music therapy devotes much energy to this process.

Through music the children can express joy, happiness, thankfulness, disappointment, fear, and confession. Ken Medema has written a beautiful song that simply states, "Sometimes I feel like sayin' how I feel." His verses express contentment, loneliness, anger, and other emotions—a fan-tastic opportunity for the child to express what he is feeling inside. Just as the Psalms are full of David's expression of emotion to God, so must our music today allow our children to express to God from their hearts. "Make a Joyful Noise" (Ingram) sings of joy and praise. "This Is The Day That the Lord Hath Made" (Sleeth) expresses gladness for each day. "Be My Lord" (Shafer) speaks of confession and commit-ment.

As we examined the biblical characteristics of worship in chapter 1, we noted that worship requires intellect and emo-tion—it is both cognitive and affective. True worship ne-cessitates affective learning. Growing up into Christ is much more than memorization of a creed or doctrinal statement. It requires attitude and character development. These are the elements of affective learning.

Music is significant in affective development because it develops aesthetic understanding. It reflects as well as determines values, feelings, thoughts, and emotions. It builds self-esteem and communicates biblical attitudes. And music speaks to and from the emotions. Music is one of God's special gifts because it can reach the inner dimensions of the personality frequently missed in much instruction. It involves the child in an expression that will remain with him long after rehearsals and programs are completed. It can significantly alter the values of the next generation for Christ.

We must understand the great potential of this ministry and not select music or plan rehearsals haphazardly. Our music must be an integrated expression of truth experienced and truth taught. Such a program will contribute substantially to the affective development of the child.

PSYCHOMOTOR DEVELOPMENT

The third area of consideration in examining the needs of the student is the area of psychomotor development. "Psychomotor learning may be defined as the acquisition, retention and transfer of voluntary movement."[4]

A distinction is often made between *movement* and *motor*.

> Movement refers to an external observable motion, while motor refers to the internal unobservable response. Movement can be involuntary. Hence, the word psychomotor is commonly used rather than motor alone to indicate that the domain of interest is movement under voluntary control of the person.[5]

Psychomotor learning exhibits voluntary control over actions and movements. It is the *doing* of the educational pyramid.

Again we need to return our biblical model to observe that growing up into Christ demands action that is the result of voluntary movement. Christ was continuously concerned that his followers put his teachings into practice. "Why do you call Me, 'Lord, Lord,' and do not *do* what I say?" (Lk. 6:46).

Christian education and music education require *doing*—a

111

voluntary physical expression of information received and attitudes felt. Music is significant in psychomotor development because it has many facets that require motor-muscular coordination and physical participation.

Initially, psychomotor development is regarded as development of the specific musical skills that make music performance possible. Carrying a tune is a physical skill. It requires first of all the ability to hear or listen accurately. Then it involves the neuromuscular control of the vocal chords to reproduce the sound that the ear heard. The ability to carry a tune is developed through the technique of tone-matching. Before a child can imitate an entire melody, he needs to be able to imitate one note—or experience a unison. We have already noted that 70 percent of the human ear develops between the ages of three and seven. Thus, we must recognize that childhood is the best time to engage the child in precision hearing. It is essential that our children learn to listen carefully. Because music education involves the development of listening skills, it has been found to be significant in both the development of tone matching and the ability of a child to follow directions. What area of education—church, school, or any other—could not benefit from increased ability to listen carefully and follow directions?

Development of vocal production is a psychomotor skill. Good vocal production requires proper respiration (breath support), phonation (control of the kind of sound that will result from the supporting breath), resonation (using the head as a proper resonating chamber so that the sound is placed properly), and articulation (pronouncing the lyrics with such precision that they may be understood by the audience). This kind of development should not be reserved for only those going into professional careers. The human voice, especially the child's voice, is a most delicate instrument. Its beauty, when used correctly, is incomparable. But when used incorrectly, a voice can be damaged for the rest of one's life.

At a music conference in southern California recently, a children's music director came with a tragic problem. What could she do for one of her nine-year-old girls who had developed nodules from imitating the voice on a current Chris-

112

tian children's record? This problem is not an isolated situation. Proper singing is a physical *skill*! It needs to be developed with our children. The techniques of proper vocal training will be discussed in chapter 11, but we need to note here that music is significant in psychomotor development because it involves voluntary motor coordination.

Ear training is also a psychomotor skill. Ear training is involved in development of the inner ear. We noted that staff reading initially is a cognitive skill. However, as one learns to read the notes, read the rhythms, and perceive the musical phrase, an ability to "hear" what the music will sound like—even before the sound is produced—will develop. For years, ear training was ignored until late high school and college formal music training. We now realize, however, that we have neglected the years when the individual is most capable of developing an "inner ear" for music—the childhood years. It is the development of this inner ear that is critical to continued involvement in music. It enables the person to sight-sing (or sight-read an instrument part). It enables a person to identify what he hears by writing it down—melodic or rhythmic dictation. And perhaps most crucial of all, it provides for the child that inner initiative to be creative—to create those melodies, rhythms, and harmonies he hears "in his head."

Rhythm participation is another psychomotor skill. Again, it is initially an imitative response. Taking the simple rhythm ♩♩♩♪ and having the children clap it, snap it, stomp it, or perform it with a patchen (thigh slapping) will aid significantly in gross motor and fine motor coordination. Extending the performance of this rhythm to the use of rhythm instruments enlarges their capacity of muscular control to the control of an object.

Instrument performance is yet another psychomotor skill. Whether it is a percussion instrument or a melodic instrument, it requires eye-hand coordination. The eye sees the rhythm or melody to be performed, and the hand engages in the necessary manipulation to produce the required sound.

Following the direction of the conductor requires psychomotor skill. Observing the entrance cues, the beat patterns, and cut-offs requires careful perception and precise execution. All of the nuances of music performance—diminishing

113

or increasing volume, accelerating or slowing tempo, perfecting phrasing, and controlling vocal production so as to achieve proper blend—all of these require the fine-motor tuning that psychomotor skill in music develops.

Writing is a physical skill and an essential ingredient in the learning process. A child who can imitate quarter notes, visualize quarter notes, perform quarter notes from visual perception, and recognize quarter notes in printed music can write quarter notes. The same is true with melodic patterns. Hearing a repeated unison note, singing a repeated unison note, and writing a repeated unison note are all integral parts of the learning process. We can begin with unison tones, proceed to diatonic patterns, and progress to interval recognition by ear, singing by sight, and writing by dictation—all with virtual ease when the process is ordered correctly. And it is the writing that ties the knot in the learning process for the child, for up until his involvement in a writing activity, the quarter notes, melodic pattern, or whatever else belongs to the teacher is part of a piece of printed material or some other nonpersonal object. Once a child has written the material, it is his. Nothing can depersonalize such an expression. This is the foundation for personal involvement and personal development!

But there is more to psychomotor development than just the functioning of neuro-muscular skills. Because music involves the child in active participation, it heightens his threshold for learning and increases his retention. Children learn by doing. A good teacher is one who will lead the children in a well-ordered sequence of activities—that the child may experience first, then learn those skills and expressions that will enhance his growth and development as a person. Music is one of God's most unique gifts because it utilizes all three domains of learning simultaneously! Take for example the rhythmic chanting of Psalm 118:24:

Such an activity involves all areas of the child's learning:

COGNITIVE   The child is memorizing Scripture.
DEVELOPMENT: The child is stating the doctrine of God's
                   creation.
                   The child is reading quarter notes, eighth
                   notes, and quarter rests.
                   The child is developing math concepts by
                   experiencing the equivalents of two
                   eighth notes and one quarter note.

AFFECTIVE   The child is involved in expressing joy
DEVELOPMENT: and gladness.
                   The child is developing a sense of trust in
                   a God who knows how to put together
                   just the right kind of day—even if it has
                   its difficulties.
                   The child is having the attitudes of joy
                   and gladness for God's creation inter-
                   nalized in his personality.

PSYCHOMOTOR   The child is developing gross motor coor-
DEVELOPMENT: dination by clapping the rhythm.
                   The child is participating in articulation
                   of the words.
                   The child is following the direction of the
                   conductor for entrance, tempo, and
                   dynamic level.
                   The child is developing an "inner ear" for
                   the relationship of quarter notes and
                   eighth notes.
                   The child is integrating the entire recita-
                   tion into the learning apparatus
                   through body involvement.
                   The child could further develop these
                   skills by taking the following rhythm in
                   rhythmic dictation: ♩ ♩ ♪♩ ♩ ♪♩ ♩│♩ ≻

All of this is evident through the fun activity of rhythmic
chant. If we add the dimension of melodic participation, we
increase each domain proportionately.

Take the following song on prayer. Since prayer is talking
to God, its title, "God-Communication," immediately sets
the stage for a personal expression to God.

God-Communication

Connie Fortunato

James R. Fortunato

Prayer is when I talk to you, And just have a good con—ver
Prayer is when I share my needs, That's part of our com-mu-ni-

sa-tion, Tel-ling you the way I feel, You don't need a long
ca-tion, Thank-ing you in ev-ery-thing, And

To Coda

ex-pla— na- tion. Prayer is when I praise your name in wor-ship and

prayerfully - rubato

116

glad a—dor——a—tion, Giv—ing all my life to you with joy, in to-tal
ded-i—ca—tion. wait-ing— wait-ing—
wait-ing—— with an——tic-i——pa——-tion.

© 1980 David C. Cook Publishing Co.

Now examine the confluent education that is taking place. (*Confluent education* is the term used to denote educational experiences that are directed to all three domains of learning and not just cognitive or affective or psychomotor.)

COGNITIVE DEVELOPMENT:

The child is stating the definition of prayer—conversation that communicates feelings, praise, adoration, commitment, and personal needs to God.

The child is acknowledging that responses to prayer are not always immediate.

The child is involved in staff reading that utilizes many intervals. He must observe the larger intervals and think how to transfer this interval jump into a vocal jump.

The child is involved in rhythmic syncopation, which he may not be able to define, but which he can identify in measures that have irregular divisions of the beat.

AFFECTIVE DEVELOPMENT:

The music creates two moods—one happy and one meditative. This speaks to the child's concept of the nature of communication with God. We should talk to him at times when we are happy—just a good conversation. We should communicate with him when we are deep in thought. Things like worship and dedication require a great deal of thought.

The expression seeks to encourage the child to speak to God just as he would a close friend—thereby helping him feel that God is his friend.

The child can feel that waiting for answers to prayer can be an exciting experience—"with anticipation"—and not drudgery as so frequently

118

communicated by prayer music that sounds like a funeral dirge. In this song the "waiting" textually and musically has a happy ending, which is designed to help the child develop the attitude that God's answers are always the right ones, even if they're not quite what we expected.

PSYCHOMOTOR DEVELOPMENT:

The child is participating in a syncopated rhythm—a natural expression for children—one they will master with great ease.

The child will especially be involved in all the areas of good tone production. It will require good respiration to reach the high notes. It will require proper phonation to create a happy sound, a meditative sound, and build anticipation. It will take proper resonation to make the notes not sound thin or squeaky, but flute-like. And it will take exceptional articulation to make sure all the words are understood clearly.

It will take precision to follow the conductor. Because of the rhythmic nature of the song, it will require fine-tuning to get all the words to sound together. Entrances and cut-offs will be critical to the vocal success, especially preceding the interlude and following the final "waiting."

It will help the child in the physical participation of expressing his feelings and needs to God. It is an aid in this kind of spiritual experience.

These observations are only surface considerations. Each area could be expanded with additional learning activities designed to focus in on additional areas. But we can observe even with this surface diagnosis that music is a powerful force in the learning of the child because it actively engages all domains of learning—cognitive, affective, and psychomotor.

SUMMARY

We noted in the first section of this book that hymn singing, psalm singing, and the singing of spiritual songs significantly affected the Christian education, worship, and evangelism of those who participated. It was hymn singing that took theology out of the creeds and placed it in the hearts of the people. It was music that perpetuated worship as a congregational expression rather than allowing it to become a clerical responsibility. It has been music that for centuries has provided man with that spontaneous expression that is able to communicate real-life experiences—whether it be ecstatic expressions of joy, encouragement for another in distress, or instruction in a highly personalized form.

Music is significant in the learning process not only because it can accommodate effectively the concerns of the teacher—readiness, motivation, and retention—but it substantially addresses the needs of the student—cognitive development, affective development, and psychomotor development. Each of these areas receives a double benefit—the benefits in development derived from the musical ingredients themselves, and the tremendous benefit from the Christian-biblical nature of the texts. Either dimension on its own would provide substantial reason for incorporating music into the education of the child, but together they blend to make one of the most dynamic forces in child development available to the person who will devote himself to establishing a credible children's music ministry.

1. Gary S. Belkin and Jerry L. Gray, *Educational Psychology*. (Dubuque, Iowa: Wm. C. Brown Company Publishers, 1977), p. 243.

2. F. David Martin and Lee A. Jacobus, *The Humanities Through the Arts*. (New York: McGraw-Hill, 1975), p. 37.

3. Thomas A. Regelski, *Principles and Problems of Music Education*. (Englewood Cliffs, New Jersey: Prentice-Hall, Inc., 1975), p. 163.

4. Belkin and Gray, *op. cit.*, p. 343.

5. *Ibid.*, p. 343.

7
Instructional Objectives

Once an instructor or programmer decides he will teach his students something, several kinds of activity are necessary on his part if he is to succeed. He must first decide upon the goals he intends to reach at the end of his course or program. He must then select procedures, content, and methods which are relevant to the objectives, cause the student to interact with appropriate subject matter in accordance with principles of learning, and finally measure or evaluate the student's performance according to the objectives or goals originally selected.
Robert F. Mager

FEW PEOPLE WOULD DENY that those who are unwilling to establish goals will seldom achieve any.

While it would probably be a misjudgment to assume that most children's music programs are conducted without some general idea of purpose—whether to provide a good musical environment for the child, or give the opportunity for performance a few times a year, or just provide for the enrichment of the children's lives through musical partic-ipation and "osmosis"—it is precisely this mind-set in music education that has reduced much music education to a low-priority, time-filling ornament. In public and private schools, many teachers bemoan the lack of cultural under-standing on the part of administrators and governing boards. Budget cuts frequently affect music programs, because they are perceived to be "nice extras" rather than significant links in the educational and developmental process of the child. While few would deny the excitement of participating in a high school marching band or choral festival, or knowing a few musical terms or skills, they are left stammering when asked to articulate specifically the worth of a music curriculum in their schools. For many, graduation from secondary school has meant the end of any musical involvement. We simply have not done a good job at making music education have life-long effects.

Churches face the same problem. Budget allocations are based on priority. Priority is based on observable and felt worth. And since many children's music programs are neither observed or felt to be substantially worthy, they are provided with "babysitting money" for budgets. A few cute programs a year simply do not merit the kind of budget allocation that a significant week-by-week program deserves.

While it is clear that a more responsible job must be done in educating pastors, church boards, school boards, and school administrators of the importance of a responsible children's music program, it is also clear that directors and music ministers need to focus their attention on clearly and specifically stating the realistic goals for a fulfilling children's music ministry, how these goals will be achieved, and how progress will be evaluated. Vague purposes produce vague results. We simply cannot expect others to recognize the worth of what we are doing when we have not taken the time to specify these goals to ourselves, our students, and our constituency.

> When music teachers can begin to show, and do so in empirical terms, the effects of their instruction on the young people who pass through the schools [or church programs], it seems ever more likely that better conditions and attitudes can be fostered. It is a question of whether music educators [or music ministers] wish to be part of the problem or part of the solution. We have contributed to the problem in the past; we can also contribute to the solution in the future.[1]

We have focused on the importance of music, biblically and educationally. We are convinced of both its intrinsic and extrinsic worth, but how do we translate this knowledge into specifically stated objectives? This chapter will establish the "how" of defining direction and establishing specific goals whereby we can both feel and observe progress.

122

ESTABLISHING LONG-RANGE GOALS

If stating that we will enrich the children's lives through musical participation is too vague, what is a satisfactory formula for communicating substantial worth? The first ingredient in a clearly stated instructional objective is the designation of the subject. In our case, it would be "a comprehensive music education program." The second element is a focus on who will be affected by our program. Certainly, the most immediate effect will be on the individual child, then the group of children, then the church (or school), and finally the community. The third ingredient, which is where the breakdown usually begins, is the outline of behaviors to be demonstrated.

Since we have established that music education is significant in the Christian maturation of the child as well as his educational development, those of us involved in a Christian children's music ministry need to focus our statements into these two categories. We have also noted that in the area of Christian maturation, there are three main areas: worship, education, and evangelism. Responsible goals will address each area. In educational development we also have three areas: cognitive, affective, and psychomotor. Again, these three areas need to be noted in terms of specific development if our program is to be regarded as substantive.

Let us formulate, then, some specific long-range objectives for a fulfilling children's music program in the church or Christian school. These objectives would state our direction for the duration of one year.

Through the incorporation of a comprehensive music education program in our curriculum, we purpose to have the following effects on the child:

Christian Maturation—Understanding that since the days of the Old Testament, thorough music training has taken place among God's people, we recognize the value of this program in three critical areas of the child's development:

Worship—Recognizing that worship is man's expression to God, we will give the child an opportunity to express to God through music the truths

123

of his character, his Word, and his creation. We will also provide encouragement for the child to express to God a personal response of dedication, adoration, confession, and petition through music.

Education—Music plays a significant role in Scripture memorization and internalization of fundamental truths. Our music selections will be focused around central themes, reflecting those doctrines we have selected for the year. The repertoire will further substantiate these themes through Scripture memorization—some with musical involvement—rhythmic and melodic; and some through recitation.

Evangelism—Realizing that Scripture commands the believer to participate in an expression of love to the world at large, we will provide for the child opportunities to share his musical expressions—both repertoire and creative musical expression—with others within the church as well as outside. We will encourage him to invite friends to participate in our program and attend our concerts. We will also take the children to various locations throughout the year where they can share their musical expressions with others who would not hear them otherwise.

These areas of Christian maturation will be demonstrated by an increased desire of the child to communicate to God in praise and commitment, and the participation of the child in creative expressions—rhythmic, melodic, and otherwise—of his personal responses to God. Internalization of fundamental truths will be observed by his ability to verbally (both musically and creatively) express the biblical truths studied, and substantiate them by Scripture memorization.

For example, the child's internalization of the doctrine of Creation will be observed by the child being able to verbalize that God is the creator of the universe—the sun, moon, stars, and all celestial bodies, and the earth and all things that exist on the earth. This expression can be by way of direct recitation or singing "All Things Bright and Beautiful," "For the Beauty of the Earth," and "This Is My Father's World." He will be able to recite Genesis 1:1; 1:31; and James 1:17.

His development in the area of evangelism will be evidenced by increased enthusiasm to participate in group programs designed to share biblical truth with people outside the church or Christian school. His personal efforts in inviting friends and neighbors will be observed, as will his personal expressions at home, school, or other involvements of the music repertoire and Scriptures learned, or creative musical expressions.

Educational Development—Realizing that music is significant in education because it involves all domains of learning—cognitive, affective, and psychomotor—we will contribute to the development of the total child with observable progress in each area.

Cognitive development—the children will learn to identify the notes on the staff by letter name. They will be able to identify quarter notes, half notes, whole notes, and eighth notes, and their corresponding rests. They will be able to identify sharps and flats that occur during the course of the song or at the beginning in the form of the key signature. They will learn to identify time signatures and count the rhythm of a given song correctly.

Affective development—Much of the affective development will center around the areas of Christian maturation and character development. Through consistent participation in repertoire of praise and thankfulness, the child will develop attitudes of thankfulness and gratefulness to God for who God is, who he (the child) is, and who others are. This perspective will contribute to the child's self-esteem, which can be observed through the expression of a healthy self-concept ("I am a unique creation of God, with special abilities and personality traits"). It will further be observed through the child's expression of appreciation for others manifested by a diminished selfishness and an expanded desire to see others express themselves. It will be further observed in increasing expressions of love for God. The area of affective development will be further addressed by selecting music that reflects biblical values and attitudes. Knowing that the world is God's creation should manifest itself by an appreciation of nature and the desire to be careful and not careless with this creation. Finally, we will address the emotional development of the child by providing expressions *to* and *from* the affective domain. Some music will express joy, some will express sadness (or repentance); some will share excitement, some will communicate thoughtfulness.

Psychomotor development—The culmination of music education into a physical expression will exhibit the following areas of development:

1. Singing—the ability to "hear" inwardly a sound and reproduce it vocally and the ability to translate specific note patterns and rhythm patterns into a melodic expression.
2. Ear training—the ability to inwardly "hear" melodic and rhythmic patterns to such an extent that the child will be able to write them from only an aural experience.
3. Composing—the ability to take certain music fundamentals (rhythmic or melodic or both) and design a creative expression.
4. Performing—a comprehensive expression of all elements of curricular ingredients designed to exhibit developed musical proficiency and communicate Christian truths.

While this kind of careful diagnosis might not be written out at the beginning of each lesson plan, it is essential that these areas of development be articulated at the outset. Such a statement will constantly determine our short-range goals, our essential ingredients, and begin to give us handles for evaluation. Long-range goals do not need to be as specific as short-range goals in terms of repertoire selections, itemized Scriptures, prevalent themes, and writing activities, but they must clearly establish our direction. Otherwise we will be tossed about from one fad to another, from one person's philosophy to another's, from the demands of one performance to the next, without ever sitting back and examining the whole, scrutinizing it carefully for comprehensive significance rather than transient expediency. Responsible music education demands articulation of goals. This is the place to begin.

ESTABLISHING SHORT-RANGE GOALS

A statement of long-range purpose is incomplete without outlining what short-range goals will provide the building blocks for such a program. Teaching a child to read is a worthwhile purpose, and yet, until it is broken down into the various elements—visual discrimination (recognizing what each letter of the alphabet looks like), auditory discrimination (distinguishing between certain sounds and knowing which letter makes which sound), and blending (putting the various sounds of the various letters together), reading is an unattainable goal. Likewise, involving our children in worship, teaching them foundational scriptural truths through music, having them memorize Scripture, learning basic musical skills, building strong character through attitude development, and participating in various musical performances are all fine substantive goals, but without the careful organizing of specific curricular ingredients focused on actualizing each of these areas, they all become elusive. All, that is, with the possible exception of performance, which is not vague or obscure. But we have already noted that this goal alone does not validate a comprehensive music education program.

The second step, then, is to take our long-range goals and break them down into small specific building blocks, each clearly recognizable by the following characteristics:

1. *Given material.* We must now be more specific than merely naming "children's choir" or "classroom music." We need to specify a particular repertoire selection, biblical truth, or fundamental music element.

EXAMPLE: "Given the hymn 'All Creatures of Our God and King' . . ."

2. *Who will be affected.* We need to specify which children—all children—the girls, boys, a small ensemble, the whole choir, or perhaps the audience.

EXAMPLE: "Given the hymn 'All Creatures of Our God and King,' each child will . . ."

3. *Aim.* This is the observable physical demonstration—the behavioral objective—which usually relates to an evidence of either cognitive, affective, or psychomotor development, whichever is appropriate to the specific activity.

EXAMPLE: "Given the hymn 'All Creatures of Our God and King,' each child will be able to identify . . ."

4. *Content.* What kind of knowledge will this behavioral objective deal with? Will it represent an acquired skill, a theological statement, or an internalized attitude or feeling response?

EXAMPLE: "Given the hymn 'All Creatures of Our God and King,' each child will be able to identify some of the evidences of God's creative power itemized in the text of the song, as well as in the Genesis 1 account."

5. *Activity.* This ingredient outlines the mental process required to exhibit the objective. It is frequently initiated by the word *by.*

EXAMPLE: "Given the hymn 'All Creatures of Our God and King,' each child will be able to identify some of the evidences of God's creative power by listing them verbally."

6. *Proficiency level.* This optional ingredient specifies criteria, when applicable.

EXAMPLE: "Given the hymn 'All Creatures of Our God and King,' each child will be able to identify some of the evidences of God's creative power by listing them verbally, and out of the eight listed in the first three verses, will be able to name at least six."

7. *Time limitation* or any *specific conditions.* Again

this is the optional specification of the conditions or limitations governing the objective.

EXAMPLE: "Given the hymn 'All Creatures of Our God and King,' each child will be able to identify some of the evidences of God's creative power by listing them verbally, and out of the eight listed in the first three verses, will be able to name at least six, preferably in proper sequence (according to the verses of the song) and in less than a minute."

It is precisely the formulation of such specific objectives that gives substance to our long-range goal of "internalizing the doctrine of Creation, and verbalizing it through appropriate repertoire selection." Our goal needs this specific building block to become attainable.

The previous example outlines a specific cognitive skill that is linked with Christian maturation in the area of education. A related instructional objective could specify affective development and link it with Christian maturation in the area of worship. The following would alter the objective in this manner:

"Given the hymn 'All Creatures of Our God and King,' each child will have an increased attitude of thankfulness and praise to God for his magnificent creation, and be able to demonstrate this attitude by taking one of the creations listed (e.g. sun, moon, wind, clouds, water, etc.) and creating a personal expression of thankfulness—whether rhythmic, melodic, or artistic—and sharing it with the class."

Note that this objective has the same essential ingredients:

1. *Given*   The hymn "All Creatures . . ."
2. *Who*   each child
3. *Aim*   will demonstrate increased thankfulness
4. *Content*   by taking one of the creations listed
5. *Activity*   and creating a personal expression, and sharing it with the class.

Because the nature of this objective does not lend itself to establishing a proficiency level or time limitation, these optional considerations were omitted.

Once we begin to operate within the specific guidelines of such objectives, we begin to see the multitudinous areas of Christian maturation and educational development that are available to us in children's music ministry. However, there is one critical difference between our observation now and our previous perception. Christian maturation and educational development are observed in specific areas, with specific evidences for all to see and evaluate, and not in vague concepts for all to "appreciate."

One of the reasons our children's music programs have been treated as fringe ornaments and not essential ministries is that we have been unwilling to clearly outline our objectives in these terms. Music appreciation and understanding at the grass-roots level is not the result of some nice euphoric feeling at the end of a good concert or program. It is, rather, the culmination of many many specific objectives—both educational (cognitive, affective, and psychomotor) and spiritual (worship, education, and evangelism) that result in the total development of the person.

ESTABLISHING SEQUENCE

The time has come to coordinate what we know in terms of child development, long-range goals, short-range goals (or instructional objectives) and our curricular calendar. Proper sequencing will help avoid two major pitfalls—one of "biting off more than we can chew" or trying to accomplish too much in too little time, and the other the exact opposite, which is more often the case in children's music programs, of taking the whole year to accomplish one or two objectives, a sure way to nurture monotony, boredom, and their correlated discipline and behavior problems.

Assuming that most children's music programs in the church and Christian school operate for nine months of the year (September to June) and involve approximately one hour per week of rehearsal (sometimes divided into two half-hour sessions), we can chart our instructional objectives in terms of weekly goals, monthly goals, multi-monthly goals (either quarterly, semester, or season), and yearly goals. Establishment of objectives in these increments will keep our focus well-balanced—one eye on achieving our specific objective and one eye on attaining our overall purpose for the year. It is this balance of perspective that will help us avoid getting off the track. Many music teachers get bogged down simply because they cannot see the end from the beginning. Sequencing helps avoid this problem.

The following presents a sample unit profile with outlined specific objectives—involving all areas of development. The example was designed for one month's work—or four lessons of one hour each.

Christian Maturation Goals:

> Scripture memorization (cognitive skill): Given the following references, Psalm 128:1 and John 13:17, each child will be able to recite the verses and identify the references correctly.

> Internalized truth (affective development): Given the biblical examples of Jonah (Old Testament) and Paul and Silas imprisoned (New Testament) each child will begin to develop a sense of trust—knowing that God's plans (and rules) for our lives are the best. This development will be exhibited by obedience to God's plans for all—to love God, to love others, to show kindness, and to forgive when we are wronged.

Educational Development Goals:

Music Literacy Skills

> Cognitive skills: Given different kinds of notes on a flashcard or overhead transparency, the child will be able to identify quarter notes, eighth notes, and half notes by naming each upon seeing it, or point to one after it has been named by the teacher. (It would be optional to add "with at least 90 percent accuracy within 30 seconds.")

> The students will begin staff reading skills by being given random notes on the staff and specifying whether the notes are "on lines" or "in spaces."

> The students will develop their staff reading skills to include middle C, D, E, F, and G. Given any of these notes, each child will be able to identify it by name or, given the name of the note, each child should be able to draw it in its correct location on the staff or select it from a group of various flashcards. Between 75 percent and 80 percent accuracy within 60 seconds would be acceptable initially.

131

Given the following musical terms—*forte, piano, crescendo, decrescendo, staccato,* and *legato,* the children will be able to define each correctly and locate them in their repertoire as they appear.

Music Repertoire Skills
(Note texts in terms of importance, lack of imagery, and relationship to the child's world)
The children will learn the following repertoire:
"I Wonder How It Felt"
"Living for Jesus"
"Take My Life and Let It Be"
"Happiness Is the Lord"
"You Don't Have to Know the Reason"
Some will be sung from memory—"I Wonder How It Felt," "Happiness Is the Lord," and "You Don't Have to Know the Reason." Others will be sung with the aid of printed words.

Affective Development: The attitude of trust is outlined in the area of Christian maturation. In addition, because of the personality of the music, it will speak to the child in terms of joy, happiness, and excitement. In so doing, the children will learn that following God's plans is not drudgery, but a joy.

Because the child is involved in a variety of types of music from different periods in history:
"Take My Life . . ." 1874
"Living for Jesus" 1917
"Happiness Is . . ." 1968
"You Don't Have to Know . . ." 1971
"I Wonder How It Felt" 1974
he can experience that trusting God and following his plans may be expressed differently by different people at different times, but each exhibits the same truth. In participating in these various expressions, the child becomes part of a body of believers that is larger than his local church and his narrow time in history. He becomes part of a historical expression that has characterized the church since its beginning.

132

Psychomotor Development: The child will exhibit vocal development by reproducing each of the tunes correctly.

The child will begin to develop eye-ear-voice coordination by singing some of the songs by note name.

The child will begin to develop an "inner ear" by recognizing certain melodic patterns (C-C-C, C-D-E, and E-D-C) by ear and being able to write them in this student workbooks.

The child will begin to develop an "inner ear" by recognizing certain rhythmic patterns:

and be able to write them in his student workbook after only hearing them.

The final area of psychomotor development is linked with Christian maturation and is evidenced by the child's participation in an act of expressing love to God, to another child, performing an act of kindness, or exhibiting forgiveness when he is wronged.

The previous outline represents comprehensive, responsible children's music ministry.[2] Each of the objectives is within the achievement level of the child and the well-organized teacher. But each objective will be realized only when we have taken time to recognize each objective. Such a procedure, while time-consuming, is also tremendously liberating. We realize in specific terms the great potential of our programs and begin to think creatively exactly how this potential can be realized.

The art of sequencing is not just a one-time operation. Formulating the objectives for the following month should seek to reinforce these same objectives but all the while building upon them. To take these same objectives and simply rehash them in different forms for the year terribly underestimates the capabilities of the child and the potential of a significant children's music program.

We have also noted that our music programs can be important building blocks not only in terms of the child's individual development, but in the spiritual development of the church and community as well. These objectives also need to be sequenced properly. Because the church is a fellowship of believers, when individuals learn to trust God and accept his patterns for living, an entire group can be affected— perhaps by parent involvement or public performance. By structuring our programs to reach into our communities we can influence the children and the homes from which they come with the same fundamentals of biblical truth.

EVALUATION

Because the church's role is "non-exclusive," that is, it does not exclude anyone regardless of his unique talents, qualities, or lack of same, we have traditionally backed away from evaluations lest in so doing we exclude someone. We have done unjustifiable damage to the spiritual development of our people by neglecting this essential ingredient. We have also severely damaged the educational responsibility to the extent that many churches are no longer even able to talk about responsible education, but rather define educational development in terms of programs offered. Evaluation is an essential ingredient if real learning is to take place.

Again we return to the quotation at the beginning of the chapter by Mager, the leading authority on establishment of instructional objectives.

> Once an instructor decides he will teach his students something, several kinds of activity are necessary on his part if he is to succeed. He must first decide upon the goals. . . . He must then select procedures, content, and methods . . . and finally measure or evaluate the student's performance according to the objectives or goals originally selected.[3]

We must note here the purpose of evaluation. First, it lets the teacher (director) and the student observe progress. Observable progress is a tremendous boost to motivation. If you want to motivate your students to continue developing, let them see how much they have accomplished! Second, it is essential in refining and adjusting our goals and objectives. In order for goals and objectives to be meaningful they must reflect observable and felt needs of the students. Only as we evaluate the accomplishment of our specific objectives and their relationship to our overall purpose are we able to continuously reaffirm the validity of our program. Third, evaluation is essential in weeding out all irrelevant material. It is not persons who are excluded but nonessential material. Finally, evaluation reinforces worth. Any program of substance will be able to withstand the rigors of evaluation. A program that has so many areas of significant contribution as a music program will not only confirm its place at the core of a school curriculum or church program, but will constantly reinforce its worthiness in areas of spiritual and educational development.

The problem arises when we take a comprehensive program such as we have just described and reduce its evaluation to surface details. How many songs did the children learn? How many musical taxonomies do the children know? How many verses did they memorize? How many children are involved in choir? While each of these questions may be indicative, to use them as the instrument measuring value fails to deal with the comprehensiveness of our purpose. Certainly a program that had as its purpose "to involve an incredible number of children" would operate with different instructional objectives than a program that had as its purpose to build biblical values and Christian character. If our purpose is going to permeate all areas of spiritual development (worship, education, and evangelism) and educational development (cognitive, affective, and psychomotor) we need corresponding evaluative measures. One cannot evaluate affective development by the recitation of cognitive skills. One cannot observe individual development in worship through outreach concerts.

Our evaluative procedures need to be commensurate with our goals. Long-range goals must undergo long-range evaluation. No one can observe the development of Christian character in four weeks of rehearsal. Short-range goals can withstand more immediate evaluations. A healthy program will incorporate each.

Evaluation of short-range goals (or instructional objectives) will fall into the areas mentioned—how many songs the children learned, how many notes on the staff they can identify, which melodic and rhythmic patterns they can write in dictation, how many verses were memorized. These are short-range goals and without them the long-range goals are obscured. But evaluation of our program does not end here.

Evaluation of long-range goals is quite another job. In terms of musical skills, do we note a development of musicianship? Instead of reading isolated notes, are the children beginning to read entire musical phrases? Is their build-up of cognitive musical skills stimulating creative expression— either in volunteer participation in rehearsal or performance, or attempting to create melodic or rhythmic expressions, or voluntarily sharing musical development at school, with friends, or with relatives? Is there a build-up of internalized fundamental truth? This area is often difficult to evaluate. However, observance of life-style—expressions of love, joy, peace, tolerance, gentleness, goodness, faith, humility, and temperance—according to Scripture, are the observable "fruit" of the Spirit. These are the tangible expressions of Christ-like character and biblical attitudes. Is the child developing in his ability to talk to God? Are our children developing the scriptural concept of self-esteem, as seen by the lessening of insecure behavior? Are our children recognizing their responsibility to share the good news of God's Word with their friends? Are we building into the lives of these children a musical and spiritual initiative that will perpetuate their involvement in the ministry of music throughout their lives?

These are some of the questions that responsible evaluation requires. This kind of a program will take careful charting. It will not be established in a week. It will take time— lots of it. But neither will its results fade away overnight. It will aid in equipping the total person for a total ministry. It will require long-range goals, short-range goals, proper sequencing, and evaluation. This is a fulfilling children's music ministry!

SUMMARY

Rather than re-state key concepts of this chapter as we have done in other chapters, we are going to involve you, the reader, in establishing your own specific goals, thereby drawing your own conclusions to this chapter. Establish these goals as if you were preparing them for a school or church administrator in an actual setting—whether or not you are currently involved in such a position.

FIRST: Define your purpose in establishing a children's choir in your church (or implementing a music curriculum in your school). What can you achieve in this year?

Now go back and mark the terms that identify your goals for Christian maturation with a red asterisk. Then check to see if you have included areas of worship, Christian education, and evangelism. Mark those that pertain to worship with a red "W", those that pertain to Christian education with a red "CE," and those that pertain to evangelism with a red "E." Go back a second time and identify the goals that relate to musical development with a blue asterisk. Designate those that relate to cognitive skills with a blue "C," those that relate to affective development with a blue "A," and those that relate to psychomotor development with a blue "P."

SECOND: Take one of the goals for Christian maturation and break it down into specific building blocks. Be sure to include the essential ingredients of a specific instructional objective: the given material, who will be affected, aim, content, activity, and proficiency level and specific conditions where they apply.

Now select one of the goals for musical development and go through the same process. Look for the same characteristics previously determined.

THIRD: Because we will be working with the specifics of sequencing a lesson plan in the next chapter, show here how you intend to build upon your specific objectives during the second month of operation. Assuming that the first statement of objective (both spiritual and musical) was to dominate your focus for the first month, how will you develop it in the second month so that you are continuing to progress toward your purpose for the year? Be sure to include areas of individual, corporate, and community benefit.

FOURTH: List here at least one means of evaluation for each objective and purpose proposed. Evaluation for objectives should be in the form of immediately observable progress. Long-range goals and purpose should be evaluated in appropriate means—character and attitude development, developed musicianship, etc.

1. Thomas A. Regelski, *Principles and Problems of Music Education.* (Englewood Cliffs, N.J.: Prentice-Hall, Inc., 1975), p. 264.

2. Connie Fortunato, *Music is for Children.* A curriculum for churches and Christian schools; Level 1. (Elgin, Illinois: David C. Cook Publishing Co., 1978), p. 7.

3. Robert R. Mager, *Preparing Instructional Objectives.* (Palo Alto, Ca.: Fearon Publishers, 1962), p. 1.

8
Teaching the Way Children Learn

Cognitive learning unfortunately has been directed mostly to the left side of the brain which deals with language, logic, reasoning and analysis. This is the adult way of learning, visual and conceptual in process. The child psyche is different. The child directs his learning more from the right side of the brain which has to do with motor-muscular, spatial orientation, artistic talents, intuition, imagination and feelings. In total he uses his entire brain, muscles and skin cells, and his five senses!
Grace C. Nash, et al.

ORGANIZING LEARNING ACTIVITIES and structuring class time has challenged the most creative teachers for centuries. If we have grasped the challenges of the teacher's considerations before learning can take place, the student's considerations in which learning takes place, and the considerations of instructional objectives that direct the areas in which learning will take place, we have begun to unveil the specifics of the educational process.

But how do children learn? What is the child's way of learning? We noted in the previous chapter that once we have established our goals, we must select procedures, content, and methods that relate to those goals. Mager, in his statement in *Preparing Instructional Objectives*, places the responsibility on the teacher (director) not only to establish the goals and select the materials, but to design the proper activities that will "cause the student to interact with appropriate subject matter in accordance with principles of learning." Simply stated, this means that in children's music ministry we must design learning activities appropriate to the way children learn.

The problem has been that for years we have taught children the way that adults learn—not the way children learn. Much music education has floundered because it bogged down in musical taxonomies—detailed musical facts—prior to the child being involved in any enjoyable music experiences. This is illustrated by the teacher who walks into music class or choir rehearsal and at some time during the rehearsal introduces "theory time" by pulling out a grand staff—10 lines, 8 spaces, treble clef, and bass clef, and states that the children are now going to learn to read music. The first step is to memorize the names of the lines and spaces in the treble clef. Of course, the lines are E-G-B-D-F (which provides the classic "Every Good Boy Does Fine"), and the spaces are F-A-C-E (which thankfully spells a word all on its own so we don't have to think up another cute saying). The fact that "good boys doing fine" has nothing to do with the notes they have sung in their song time is not even considered a valid point of question. This kind of concern, however, is not tangent to the point, it is the point. Such approaches to music instruction are needless obstacles, similar to giving a ten-month-old baby a pair of crutches so he can learn to walk!

Such an approach not only is contrary to the child's way of learning, it actually produces skills arrest, which is developing proficiency to a certain point and then hitting a dead end. Many people throughout our society have been exposed to some kind of music instruction during their lifetime. Many can recite "every good boy does fine." But since the bass clef was different—"Good boys do fine always," and "All cows eat grass" or "All cars eat gas"—they can't remember which is which, and in the end decide either they can't read the bass clef or they can't read music at all! What a tragic commentary, especially when the musical alphabet is so simple: A-B-C-D-E-F-G. This information is always correct, and will apply in the treble clef, the bass clef, the tenor clef, the alto clef, or any other clef.

Recent approaches in music education have sought to reverse this problem. They need to be congratulated for their efforts. Many have reacted so adversely to this approach,

141

however, that they have eliminated literacy skills and musical taxonomies altogether. They only try to involve the child in enjoyable music experiences. While we need to alter our approach, it is also essential that we include all elements of learning, which includes literacy. It is not the ingredients we need to change but the sequence and method with which they are presented.

A good teacher is neither an information dispensary spitting out musical information at regular intervals nor a musical model engaged in the production of musical clones, but a guide who will lead the children through properly sequenced musical experiences, provide supporting information along the way coupled with good musical examples, and stimulate the child to incorporate this total expression of music into his person in such a way that his expressions are personal and creative, and his life is enriched. It is precisely this well-ordered sequence of experiences that constitutes the procedures, content, and method. And it is the design of these experiences that forms the focus of this chapter.

EXPERIENCING PITCH

Many of the children who come into our children's choirs and music classes will already be able to carry a tune. With the advent of children's television—Sesame Street and Mr. Roger's Neighborhood—even children who might not otherwise be sung to are now the recipients of musical experiences at a very young age. But what about the child who does not sing or carry a tune? Do we place him in musical isolation and tell him to open his mouth but not make any sound because he doesn't sing the right notes? Or do we place him in another activity—tetherball or crafts—and tell him not to worry, that not all children are "musically inclined"? Such approaches, more common than any of us would like to admit, can only damage a child's self-esteem and deprive him of one of the most natural human expressions—the gift of music.

We have already established that singing is a physical skill. It requires auditory discrimination—hearing a sound correctly—and the ability to work the vocal cords in such a way as to control the sound they produce and create the same sound that was heard. It is common knowledge that gross-motor and fine-motor control develop differently with each individual. We can't predict when a baby will be able to walk, drink from a cup, write his name correctly, etc. If a child does not walk on his first birthday, we don't immediately assume that he is not "inclined to walking" and give him up as an ambulatory failure. Nor if a child does not write his name correctly the first day he enters kindergarten do we assume that he is not "inclined" to be literate! In each case we realize our responsibility to provide increased exposure (practice) and encouragement (motivation) and assistance (teaching).

The same principle holds true with singing. Simply because a child does not carry a tune by the time he enters kindergarten or first grade does not mean he should be scrapped as "nonmusical." Many times this is the result of physical immaturity. Some children just have not developed their fine-motor control to a sufficient extent that they can carry a tune. Others have had deprived musical environments—they have not been sung to enough to stimulate sufficient practice at making a musical response. Most of these children with a little practice (increased musical environment), encouragement and some practical teaching techniques will develop into fine singers—at least able to carry a tune, participate in an ensemble, and gain some self-satisfaction.

Sometimes there are psychological barriers to singing. Frequently children confuse the concepts of "high" and "low." Instead of thinking of them in terms of pitch, they think of them in terms of volume. This is the result of environmental conditioning—"Turn the TV down, it's up too high!" Then there is the child that has been told by adults that he can't sing. Since behavior usually conforms with image, he is convinced he can't, and therefore he doesn't. Sometimes children are not interested in singing because of lack of interest. Many children "don't like music" simply because they think that those who like music have to sit still and sing for an hour. Regardless of the activity, nothing is exciting enough to warrant sitting still for an hour! Once they participate in music that may be marching to a drum-beat, participating in a rhythm ensemble—or doing something other than what

143

they thought was boring, they find out they like music just fine! Some children are afraid to sing—they are perhaps intimidated by the director, their peers, their parents, or perhaps cannot even isolate the cause of the fear—but nonetheless they are afraid.

The last cause of inability to sing is physical abnormality—perhaps a hearing defect. This will require different treatment than the approaches we will be describing. This kind of problem should be cared for with medical treatment and the prescribed treatment of a professional. All the other problems, however, should be helped substantially with one or a combination of the following approaches. With a pleasant environment and patient instruction, a child's inability to sing in tune should disappear sometime during the elementary school years.

The first activity in learning to carry a tune is to experience a unison. This can be approached in a variety of ways. One way is to sing a word or short phrase to the child on one note, and ask them to be your echo. Be sure to choose a note that is in their comfortable range—about F#. You might try:

la, la,   la   How are you   to-day?

If they echo you correctly, you can go on to the next step. If they do not, then reverse the game and ask them to sing a sound to you—any sound. Then the teacher should match it! In so doing, the child's experience of a unison is just as accurate. Ask the child to do it again—maybe change the syllable or sentence—just to reinforce the fact that he can experience a unison correctly. Then ask him to listen while you sing the same note to him. Be sure to use the same tone he selected—and then have him be your echo.

In most cases, this first step of tone-matching will be accomplished by experiences of this nature. If not, you may want to do some vocal exercises—simply demonstrating the flexibility of the voice—and letting the child feel what muscles he uses to control the sound. The use of body involvement will also help make the concept of "going up" or "coming down" concrete. There are many such exercises—making your voice an elevator and starting on the bottom floor and going up, making your voice a ladder or staircase, or even a fire-engine siren. The use of the Curwen hand signs (used in Kodaly music instruction) are also very helpful in helping a child visualize what it is his voice must do. (They are also tremendously helpful in the teaching of melodies.)

Once a child has experienced a unison and can match a tone, the next step is to begin singing intervals. The easiest interval for a child to sing is the descending minor third. (It is the predominant interval in "Ring-a-round the Rosey.") Actually, once a child can match a pitch, it is easier for him to sing this interval than continue on a unison sustained tone. This interval opens the possibility of many games, from "name-singing" to "calling the roll." You might establish the pitch, and ask the children to sing their names to you:

Or, you might try taking the roll this way (using a major third rather than a minor third):

After the children have done this successfully (especially if they are preschool age) they might enjoy making up some echo games of their own. Other opportunities for expanding this experience are question and answer games, which give the child more opportunity for creativity than echo games that simply call for imitation.

EXPERIENCING STAFF READING

We mentioned that one of the psychological barriers preventing children from singing in tune is confusion of the concept of "high" and "low." The same confusion is raised in understanding staff reading—what is "up" and "down"? The following simple activity will help eliminate the confusion and aid in both tone-matching and staff reading.

> Stretch as high as you can reach, and invite the children to join you. Then quickly swoop your hands down to the floor. Do this several times, and then ask the children to make their voices match their body movements. As you stretch high, make your voice go high; then lower your voice as you swoop down. Go back and forth several times, and then stop.
>
> Tell the children you are going to play a *listening game*. If the sounds you (or your pianist) play on the piano are high, you want them to reach way up. If they are low, you want them to bend over and touch the floor.
>
> Use any melody pattern you like—"Jesus Loves Me" or "The Farmer in the Dell," or improvise your own. Play in the highest octaves of the piano, then in the lowest, until all the children are doing the correct gestures. Then gradually increase your octave changing, until you only play up high or down low for two or three beats.[1]

You could amplify the activity by using different instruments of the orchestra, or a xylophone. Be sure to include some notes that are low in pitch but loud in volume, and vice versa. This will help reinforce the fact that they need to think in terms of pitch rather than volume. If the low notes are soft and the high notes are loud, the confusion will not be remedied. There are any number of ways to vary this experience, all with the same result—to help the child *experience* the difference between "high" and "low," "treble" and "bass," "ascending" and "descending"—all basic prerequisites for learning to read the staff. Once the children have experienced these concepts, it is easy to add the terms "treble" and "bass" and show them the corresponding musical signs—treble clef and bass clef.

Another area that causes confusion in staff reading is the fact that we give the children a staff—or even a partial staff and begin calling these

 "in the space" notes, and these

"on the line" notes. We never take into consideration that most of these are school-age children who have just mastered the art of printing or writing their letters "on the lines"—ᴀ ᴇ ᴏ ɪɪ. A student who was asked to write the letter "O" or a circle on this line would carefully draw ◯◯◯. To draw ⊖⊖⊖ would certainly show carelessness, and be met by encouragement to "keep the bottom of the letter from dipping down below the line." But when they come to music, it is just the opposite: This ⊖⊖⊖ is "on a line," and this ◯◯◯ is "in a space." And yet we glibly throw out ten lines, eight spaces, and tell them that "every good boy does fine."

Rather than taking ten or fifteen minutes to explain verbally what each designation means (we must remember that children don't learn by our explanations—they learn by *doing*), it is much more meaningful to build the correct musical definitions into their *experience*. There are many approaches that use chalkboard, overhead transparency, and flashcards. But initially, one of the most fun ways can be to use the child's body—build it into his *own physical experience*. Before the children come to class or rehearsal, simply place five straight masking-tape lines on the floor (or if you have room, you can put all ten). Place them about eighteen inches apart. You may even add the clef signs. When it is time for them to participate in this activity:

> Ask the children to stand on one of the lines you have put on the floor. Explain that the tape should go right under the middle part of their feet (not their toes or heels) but the MIDDLE!
> Then ask them to move to the space between the lines. This time they shouldn't be touching the tape at all—their feet are in the space. Go back and forth slowly so each child experiences what it means to be on a line or in a space. Gradually increase your speed, until you can count, "On a line, one, two, three. In a space, one, two, three." After they are good at this exercise, ask them to return to their seats.[2]

Once their experience is accurate, you can ask them to transfer the activity to an overhead transparency—either using pre-formed notes and asking them to place their note on a line or in a space, or you may wish to have them draw notes on the lines or in the spaces. For younger children you may assist them by placing the dots for the note in the space ⎯ ⌒ ⎯ and having them trace it. Or you may wish to have them use individual staves in a student workbook or on a piece of construction paper and place notes on lines or in spaces. These notes could be pre-cut from black construction paper or children could even use small cubes, which are easy and fun to manipulate.

This activity builds into the experience of the child an additional concept that at first doesn't meet the eye. Children who walk through the experience of stepping on the lines and then in the spaces build into their understanding that neighboring notes are in alternate positions, i.e., if "E" is on a line, then the note next to it—in this case "F"—is in a space. Although identification of specific notes will come at a later stage, this concept of diatonic progression alternating between line and space is often hard for the children to grasp. Sometimes they want to progress from one line to the next or from one space to the next in order to arrive at the next note.

Once the children understand—by experience—what it means to be on a line, in a space, and proceed to neighboring locations, the only information needed to read the complete staff is the musical alphabet—A, B, C, D, E. F, G. Once these letters are "plugged in" to any location, the child can ascend, descend, jump intervals, sing by note name, or any other staff-reading project. The bass clef will not be any more difficult than the treble clef—it uses the same alphabet and moves from line to space just as the treble clef. They will probably want to form a few "landmarks" in their mind, such as middle C, treble G, bass F, treble C, bass C, or "first-line E" on the treble clef and "bottom-line G" on the bass clef. Any one of these techniques will help the child "plug in" correctly, and from there, he can handle it on his own.

This kind of a foundation is time-consuming. But there are many benefits. It involves active participation! It is always accurate and will not need to be modified in another year or two to make it "more correct" musically speaking. It is fun! It can be adjusted to suit many different age levels. This is experience first—then learn!

148

EXPERIENCING RHYTHM

From the days that toddlers bounce up and down while holding their crib railing, children express rhythm. Young children are naturally rhythmic. In fact, their rhythmic precision is often more accurate than adults' because of their developing ear. But how do we take this natural expression and give it substance so that it might be further developed throughout life and give new impetus to creative expression rather than simply dissipating as the maturation process continues? Children who are very rhythmic at young ages can lose this gift completely if it is not in some way tied to meaningful experiences that will stimulate development.

Many teachers like to use rhythm instruments. They are fine, but they are inanimate objects and will not incorporate rhythmic experience into the learning apparatus of the child as quickly as the use of body percussions. There are four basic body percussions that are used extensively by many music educators who work with children—the clap, snap, patchen (thigh-slapping), and stomp. Because these involve the motor-muscular control of each child, they are participating in kinesthetic or "feeling" learning. Another advantage is that these are each very personal "instruments" that can be taken home with each child—they do not have to turn them in to be stored in the cabinet until the next class time. Use of physical participation frequently cuts down or eliminates excess verbal explanation on the part of the teacher—they simply learn by doing. Frequently it is advantageous to begin a class with little or no explanation. This immediately focuses their attention on the director and gets them involved.

> After the children are seated, begin clapping a steady beat of quarter notes without any explanation. They will join you almost immediately. If they don't, encourage them to do so. After a moment or two, switch to snapping, then to a patchen (slapping your thighs with the palms of your hands). You can include a foot stomp if you desire.
>
> Just when the rhythm is really going well, stop instantly by putting your hands up in the air. Stand there silently until everyone has stopped. Then begin again, stopping shortly afterward.
>
> This time the class should be watching more closely, although you will probably have a few stragglers. Now begin a steady beat

again, but continue to shorten it, until you end up with the pattern ♩♩♩♪ . Clap it, then stop, holding your hands up in the air. After a time or two of ♩♩♪♩|♩♩♩♪ they will catch on.

When you have obtained precision, ask the children to be your echo and add pitch to your game (any pitch as long as the interval is a descending minor third).

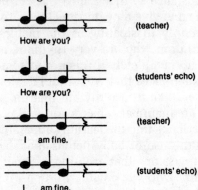

How are you? (teacher)

How are you? (students' echo)

I am fine. (teacher)

I am fine. (students' echo)

Continue with other sentences or sentence fragments, such as "I am glad" and "You are here."[3]

This kind of experience can be expanded to give the children opportunity for creative responses, or altering the rhythm for different answers.

How are you?

I'm fine.

I know.

Swaying to music, marching, tapping one's shoulders, playing choo-choo train—these are only a few of the possibilities for designing activities that will allow the child to internalize specific rhythmic patterns. Once a child has experienced the rhythm and expanded it through various uses (some imitative and some creative) it is no longer a threat to have him *visualize* the rhythm. It is only providing written symbols for something he has already done—success

150

motivation. Without the addition of this dimension—
visualization of specific rhythmic symbols—the child's experience remains simply that—a nice fun "game." Until it is
tied to substantive learning it cannot be further developed,
nor does it retain meaning beyond the individual activity,
nor can it be transferred to other music learning. Once he
learns to recognize a quarter note visually, however, he can
identify it in a church hymnal, a collection of children's
songs, a note in instrumental music, or any other place he
finds one. Because his experience has been tied to meaningful learning, it becomes transferable to all areas of music
involvement.

EXPERIENCING TEXT

Teaching the words to songs seems to be an area where
many directors have difficulty. Many avoid a potential problem by selecting songs with repetitive simple texts. Yet it
hardly seems fair to deprive children of interesting songs
with interesting texts just because we don't know how to
teach them the words. Many take the "drill" approach, facing their "troops" with military precision and discipline—
going over and over and over until we think it almost impossible for them to forget, but scared to death that they
might. Our fears are justified. While repetition and reinforcement are important ingredients in retention, more important
is the significance of the original meaning. It is futile to
repeat over and over again strings of meaningless words that
have not been related to the child's life and way of learning.
We must also remember that retention is directly proportional to the involvement of the three domains of learning—
psychomotor, affective, and cognitive. But how can we build
text into the child's way of learning—experience first?

There are several ways to relate texts to the child's experience. Some use pictures, body gestures, or questions. Each of
these will work fine with certain songs. Children who are
learning "The Lord's My Shepherd" (Crimond) may be
helped by selecting pictures of a shepherd, green pastures
with quiet water, a dark valley, and a banquet table. In fact,
some music teachers of young children teach exclusively
with visualized songs. This again is evidence that much of
our teaching is oriented to the way adults learn, not the way

children learn. While visualization may help children remember some songs, we must remember that the visual-conceptual way of learning is directed mostly to the left side of the brain (adult learning) while the child's way of learning is directed more from the right side of the brain—or motor-muscular participation.

Relating songs to body gestures is an excellent way to incorporate text and sequence into the learning by involving body participation. Take Psalm 107:1, which we illustrated in chapter 6. These words could be spoken in the suggested rhythm, or they could be further incorporated into the child's learning by body participation.

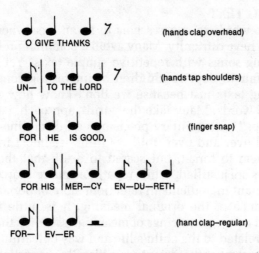

Another way to involve the children in experiencing text is to involve them in sequencing the phrases from the verse. The following activity represents one possible way to teach the first verse to "The Star Carol" by Alfred Burt—a beautiful Christmas selection.

Divide the class into four groups. Distribute four cards [previously prepared squares of paper with the text broken down into phrases—one phrase per square] with the words from the first verse of "The Star Carol." Give one card per group, starting from left to right. Ask each group to read their card aloud, calling on them in the correct order.

Go through the verse several times, with each group reading their own phrase. Then see if they can recite their phrase without looking at the card. If they can, switch the cards around so that each group has a new card, distributing them from right to left this time. Repeat the game. Continue this until each group has had each of the four cards. By the third and fourth times, they should know the order, so ask each group to come in at the proper moment. Then see how many can recite the entire verse from memory with you.[4]

Of course songs that use repetitive phrases such as "Jesus, We Just Want to Thank You" are mastered very quickly. Songs that have direct repetition such as the German Christmas carol, "How Great Our Joy," should have the echo sections extracted and taught first. That insures immediate success—and when it comes time to learn the various introductory phrases, the children will already feel they know the majority of the song. You could approach the new selection by an "echo game."

Tell the children you are going to play an echo game with them, reminding them what an echo does. Then sing:

and have them echo you. Next sing:

and have them echo you.

Then sing:

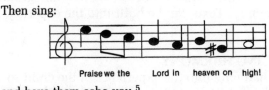

and have them echo you.[5]

This is not to say that sometimes song texts cannot be taught by rote. Definitely they can—and should be. One of

153

the benefits of good music instruction is that it teaches children to listen more carefully. There are occasions when they should be asked to listen as the director or teacher sings an entire verse to a song and then asks them to join in on whatever parts they remember. However, this approach does not suit all songs—nor does it involve the children in a variety of learning activities. Since each child learns differently, we must remember to avoid ruts and not teach the same things in the same way all the time. Remember, a good teacher is one who is always looking for new ideas.

Some song texts lend themselves to breaking down into short sections and dividing the class into corresponding sections. By dividing texts into short easily-mastered units, with each group responsible for only one unit of text, we again stimulate musical motivation by insuring success and placing it within the achievement range of each child. Then when the units are re-assigned, the children have participated in each section (psychomotor involvement), feel successful (affective learning), and can recite all sections (cognitive learning).

Other songs can be related to the child's world through meaningful questions or stories. The song "I Wonder How It Felt" will be remembered easily when linked with the story of Jonah and the fish, Paul and Silas in jail, David and Goliath, and Moses in the bullrushes. Texts that relate scriptural paraphrases can be enhanced through memorizing the scriptural basis of the song.

There are many ways to teach text—and all of them can be meaningful and yet fun. The specific song will determine the experience—echo, sequence, short phrases, pictures, questions, association, imitation, or recitation. Remember to involve all parts of the learning process, learn by doing, and do things differently. Texts can be built into the experience of the child!

EXPERIENCING HARMONY

Building harmony into the experience of the child so that he is capable of melodic and rhythmic independence is the basic prerequisite for part-singing. Translating this desirable musical goal into specific activities for children may seem a bit unrealistic, but it need not be. Children are capable of singing in harmony—beautiful harmony. The sound of children's voices singing in precision harmony is an unparalleled beauty. Choirs like the Vienna Boys Choir and the Korean Orphan Choir have thrilled audiences all over the world. Are their accomplishments achieved by musical prodigies or just fine children who have been through the well-ordered sequence of good musical training, including singing in harmony?

Children all over the world—in your town and mine—are capable of singing in harmony if we build in the proper sequence of activities. Remember, children are not born with musical prowess; it is developed.

One of the easiest ways to introduce the children to the concept of harmony—the fact that two parts can exist at the same time—is by involving them in rhythm ensembles of more than one part, and have each child chant his or her part. One part should be a repetitive phrase—usually called an "ostinato." The second part operates above the ostinato. We have used the Scripture "O give thanks unto the Lord, for he is good, for his mercy endureth forever" several times in our illustrations. This could easily be made into an elementary "harmonic" rhythm ensemble by creating an ostinato that simply chants:

♩ ♩ ♩ 𝄾 ♩ ♩ ♩ 𝄾 ♩ ♩ ♩ 𝄾

O GIVE THANKS,   O GIVE THANKS,   O GIVE THANKS, etc.

The second group performs the previously illustrated rhythmic chant above it. It will be executed most easily by bringing in the ostinato first, then adding the second group, letting the second group finish their chant, and finally ending with the ostinato again.

A second approach is the use of dialogue songs. In dialogue songs usually the choir is divided into two groups—each singing its part independently—one right after the other, with only a few vocal overlaps to create harmony. An example of this kind of song is the finale of the children's musical *The Enchanted Journey*. "Blessing and Honor" takes the form of a dialogue with the two voices answering each other as in a conversation. While such selections may not develop extensive harmonic experience, they do encourage vocal independence.

A third way is through the use of descant. It is often delightful to take a song with which the children are very familiar and have the director (or perhaps an instrument) add a descant. Then have a few of the children join in singing the optional part while the majority remain on the familiar melody. This insures security of the original melody. During successive class times you may rotate the children who participate in the descant singing to provide each child the opportunity to create the harmony.

Rounds and canons provide excellent opportunities for initial harmonic participation. The approach would be similar to that of descant involvement. Have the entire class comfortable with the melody before you confuse them by adding another part. Initially add the second part by using only a few children—or perhaps only the leader. Gradually add to it until each group is of equal strength. Even though some rounds are designed for three and four parts, it is wisest to only begin with two.

Sometimes two sections of a song—verse and chorus—may have the same harmonic structure and can be fit together nicely to form harmony. "Sing Noel" by Natalie Sleeth offers such an example. After the second verse and chorus, she forms two parts by having one group sing the third verse while another group is singing the chorus simultaneously. Then when the group that is singing the verse gets to the chorus, the group that began with the chorus switches to the verse. By teaching the entire class the verse and chorus, they automatically learn both parts.

Other times a song may be comprised of two parts—nonsequential in terms of verse-chorus, but harmonious—and each a distinct melody. The song "Be My Lord," by Carolyn Shafer has this characteristic. The song is composed of two distinct parts—an upper melody and a lower melody. In such cases, it is wisest to decide on which melody you will teach the class first and teach it to the entire class. Once they know it, the director can sing the second part so the children get accustomed to hearing it. Then teach the second melody to the entire class, and have the director sing the first melody. Have a few children join the director. Switch the melodies back and forth a few times to develop security.

156

Gradually divide the groups so they are of equal strength.

Another way to teach children to sing in harmony is by actual chord and triad singing. After the children have learned to read the notes on the staff (which should be fairly soon in their music education) and have taken some simple melodic dictation, melodic recognition, and sight-singing by note-name, you might try the following activity.

Divide the class into three groups, and have each group imitate you: group 1 should sing C-C-C-C-C, group 2—E-E-E-E-E, group 3—G-G-G-G-G. Then tell them to sing their phrase again, this time holding their note after you have gone on to the next group.

Place the following overhead transparency on the screen:

Tell group 1 you want them to sing the notes on top, connected by a dotted line. Ask them to identify the note names, the pitch—it goes up a second and then back to where it started—and then have them sing it.

Group 2 is to sing the middle notes, connected by a solid line. Go through the same process with them.

Group 3 is to sing the bottom notes, connected by the wavy line. Again go through the same process so each group knows its notes and what happens to the pitch. Then sing it all together as you point to the triads.[6]

The same activity can be expanded to include:

and finally

Although this activity may not correlate directly to one of the songs in their repertoire, it does build the children's harmonic experience, increase vocal independence, and stimulate the inner ear's harmonic development.

ESTABLISHING CURRICULUM

The preceding pages have illustrated only a few of the

possibilities for involving children in meaningful musical experiences. "Experience first—then learn" is not a lofty philosophy. It is the concrete way of learning. It is the child's way of learning. Once we understand this, we need to know how to properly sequence learning experiences so they contribute to an orderly build-up of knowledge—and not merely assorted activities.

Each of the examples given takes only the first step of the experience process. After involving the children in this kind of experience, they need to visualize what they have been doing. Visualization is the first step in tying their experience to comprehensive learning. After the children have participated in clapping or snapping ♩♩♩𝄾 the teacher can show them what the rhythm looks like by writing it on the chalkboard, overhead projector, or flashcard. As she draws the rhythm, she can identify the substance, "Quarter note, quarter note, quarter note, rest." Then have the children read it aloud with the director as she points, "Quarter, quarter, quarter, rest."

Next combine their visualization with experience. This will reinforce that what they are seeing really isn't new—they've already done it several times. It is only adding a written symbol to what they know. The teacher may even select a "conductor" from among the children and have him point to the notes while she plays the piano, or she may opt to point to the notes while she taps her hand against her thigh and asks the children to tap along as a suitable recording is being played.

Once this has been achieved, the children are ready for expansion, or their first opportunity for transfer. Simply stated, transfer is the ability to take the material that has been learned and re-apply it in a different situation. If the children have experienced and visualized ♩♩♩𝄾 , then the next step is to ask what they think ♩𝄾 ♩𝄾 would sound like. The child could clap or snap what he thinks the rhythm should sound like because it only requires that he take the information he has just experienced and visualized and rearrange it. Give the entire class the opportunity to participate in the transfer. A class could even be divided into two groups—one for ♩♩♩𝄾 and one for ♩𝄾 ♩𝄾. This could be reinforced as a "question-answer" game. Or the same material could be expanded even further to ♪ ♩ ♩ ♪ , with the same approach—"What do you think this would sound like?"

Transfer or expansion cannot be sustained too long, or the "stretching" experiences become too much work. After one or two opportunities for transfer, go back and reinforce the material in its original and expanded form. Reinforcement can take the form of repetition, or partial repetition—where the experience is repeated but the accompaniment is altered. It is best to design several types of activities at the reinforcement stage of learning.

Once the children are secure with the information, they are ready to write the material. The teacher would ask the children to write what they hear, and then clap ♩ ♩ ♩ ♪ . Because what they "heard" and what they "experienced" were identical, the child is really only filling in the visualization step—and combining it with his own fine-motor coordination skills. It is the writing process that solidifies the material in the child's mind because it combines all of the steps and makes them personal. He has combined his experience, visualization, transfer, and reinforcement.

Writing paves the way for composition and creativity. The writing adds the personal dimension to the musical meaning. It cannot be overlooked without damaging musical development. Creativity, the personal expression of the individual, is one of the greatest benefits of music education. Not only does it provide an expression *to* the child of cognitive and affective material, but it is an expression *from* the child of his inner person. Without carefully sequencing a child's musical experiences so he actually learns, meaningful creativity and composition are not possible. Creativity does not happen in a vacuum. It requires exposure (experience), stimulus (motivation), and meaning (learning).

One must also remember that without clear instructional objectives, isolated musical experiences become so much assorted music miscellany. Many teachers are able to think up cute musical games. But unless they are tied in *substance and sequence* to a clearly stated goal, they become no more meaningful than games at a birthday party. While it is tragic to see some music learning killed by the director who stands and lectures to the children for an hour or teaches them only by rote, it is equally meaningless in terms of real learning for children to participate in cute musical games that don't lead anywhere. The worth of these experiences lies in their ability to help us proceed to our goal of increased musical development, involvement, and enrichment.

Comprehensive curriculum is the combination of clearly stated *objectives, procedures* (experiences that are tied in substance and sequence to the objectives), *materials* (the content used in the experiences), and *evaluative devices* (feedback opportunities). The absence of one ingredient calls the title into question. Many music materials endeavor to earn the title "curriculum" when they should be properly designated as "materials" only. Such is true for song collections, record collections, theory workbooks, and activity collections. While many of these are good *materials*, they do not exemplify comprehensive *curriculum*. Responsible music education in the church and Christian school demands the inclusion of each element. To reduce the standard is beneath our responsibility as musicians and as Christians.

PRACTICAL PARTICIPATION PAGES

The following exercises have been designed to help you incorporate the principles discussed so far into practical lesson plans by taking you through the various steps of lesson design, and asking you to complete each step.

1. Select a scriptural theme that you feel is important for your group of children to internalize. Be as specific as possible. State what you would like them to know (cognitive knowledge), what you want them to feel (affective knowledge), and what kinds of behavior or observable demonstrations (psychomotor learning) will be your goal.

2. Select appropriate Scripture memorization to substantiate your biblical theme. Be sure the text (and version) you use can be understood by the children you are working with.

3. List three possible repertoire selections (more if you can). One should be a hymn, one a psalm (or Scripture song), and one a spiritual song. Remember the text should be important, avoid imagery, and be relevant to the child's world. The music should be interesting and appropriate for the text.

4. Design an appropriate instructional objective for one lesson in each of the following areas: biblical theme, Scripture memorization, repertoire singing, and music fundamentals.

5. Select two of your instructional objectives and design experiences in which the children can participate to help them achieve your goal.

6. For the two experiences described above, create an opportunity for feedback or evaluation that will indicate when and how you know that your objective has been achieved.

1. Connie Fortunato, *Music is for Children*. A curriculum for churches and Christian schools; Level 1. (Elgin, Illinois: David C. Cook Publishing Co., 1978). p. 9.

2. *Ibid.*, p. 10.

3. *Ibid.*, pp. 7-8.

4. *Ibid.*, p. 67.

5. *Ibid.*, p. 70.

6. *Ibid.*, p. 143.

Bibliography
for Part Two

Alderson, Richard. *Complete Handbook of Voice Training.* West Nyack, New York: Parker Publishing Company, Inc., 1979.

Belkin, Gary, and Gray, Jerry. *Educational Psychology.* Dubuque, Iowa: Wm. C. Brown Company Publishers, 1977.

Bloom, Benjamin S., ed. *Taxonomy of Educational Objectives.* New York: David McKay Company, Inc., 1956.

Burnett, Millie. *Melody Movement and Language.* San Francisco, California: R and E Research Associates, 1973.

Fortunato, Connie. *Music Is For Children.* Level 1. Elgin, Illinois: David C. Cook Publishing Co., 1978.

Frost, Joe L., and Kissinger, Joan B. *The Young Child and the Educative Process.* New York: Holt, Rinehart and Winston, 1976.

Garretson, Robert L. *Music in Childhood Education.* Englewood Cliffs, New Jersey: Prentice-Hall, Inc., 1976.

Mager, Robert F. *Preparing Instructional Objectives.* Palo Alto, California: Fearon Publishers, 1962.

Martin, F. David, and Lacobus, Lee A. *The Humanities Through the Arts.* New York: McGraw-Hill Book Company, 1975.

Nash, Grace C. *Creative Approaches to Child Development with Music, Language and Movement.* New York: Alfred Publishing Co., Inc. 1974.

Nash, Grace C., Jones, Geraldine W., Potter, Barbara A., and Smith, Patsy S. *The Child's Way of Learning.* Sherman Oaks, California: Alfred Publishing Co., Inc., 1977.

Newman, Grant. *Teaching Children Music.* Dubuque, Iowa: Wm. C. Brown Company Publishers, 1979.

Nye, Robert Evans, and Nye, Vernice Trousdale. *Music in the Elementary School.* Englewood Cliffs, New Jersey: Prentice-Hall, Inc., 1977.

Nye, Vernice. *Music for Young Children.* Dubuque, Iowa: Wm. C. Brown Company Publishers, 1975.

Regelski, Thomas A. *Principles and Problems of Music Education.* Englewood Cliffs, New Jersey: Prentice-Hall, Inc., 1975.

Thatcher, David A. *Teaching, Loving, and Self-directed Learning.* Pacific Palisades, California: Goodyear Publishing Company, Inc., 1973.

Part Three

CONTEMPORARY CHALLENGES

9
Organizing an Effective Children's Music Program

We have been talking about ourselves and the importance of our work, but it is time now to organize the choir program. Unless you plan carefully the program can easily fail. It is not enough to want a program; you must spend time and effort getting your entire church enthusiastic about it. Perhaps you are enthusiastic to the bursting point, but does the rest of the church share your enthusiasm? It takes time to get everybody interested, informed, and moving with you; so you must make plans to talk with a number of people.
Madeline D. Ingram

WITHOUT A WORKABLE ORGANIZATION, our fantastic ideas and dynamic potential remain on bookshelves—left to gather dust.

What are the organizational aspects necessary to put a children's music program into operation? What must be done before potential is translated into practice; concept into the concrete?

PERSONNEL—LEADERSHIP
Of utmost importance is the supportive ministry of the pastor (or school administrator) and the governing board. It is not enough to have their tacit approval. Unfortunately, some leaders have an "out of sight—out of mind" philosophy toward children's ministry. They are willing to give blanket approval to our ideas as long as we generate the

energy to carry them out.

The pastor not only needs to approve your program, he needs to internalize your goals. The school administrator needs to do more than fill a music position; he needs to understand the direction of his music person. This kind of coordination of purpose should be the result of extended communication—talk, interact, share your goals, share your curriculum. Give him every reason to *want* to support both you personally and your program. This kind of support is crucial to the effectiveness of the children's music ministry.

School boards and church boards are important factors in establishing an effective organization. It is these boards that formulate and evaluate direction. They frequently are responsible for sensing the needs of the people and translating these needs into effective solutions. They usually control budget or at least make budget recommendations. The communication you have established with your pastor or administrator needs to be transmitted to these boards. Their understanding of your overall purpose as well as specific objectives will help them understand precisely how your program will minister to many of the needs of the community. As they see these goals accomplished it will encourage the allocation of additional budget.

Many churches operate with a music committee. Certainly these people need to be among your most ardent supporters. They need not only to understand and support your program, they need to help publicize it to the church family. Children's music ministry should be a frequent agenda item for their meetings—always discussing new ways to support your ministry—in terms of budget, leadership, facility, equipment, exposure, and public ministry.

Many churches also have a music minister. Sometimes the children's music director and the music minister are the same person. If not, your music minister should be your closest consultant, counselor, and confidant. Good communication will serve to enhance the total music ministry in the church. Share the burdens of each other's ministry—pray together. Ask his advice on difficult decisions. Keep him informed about the areas of your program that are encouraging as well as those that need attention. Have him help in leadership recruitment, interviewing, and training. Support his leadership. Remember, you are part of the same ministry. Divisiveness can only create conflict.

School administrators need to present their music teacher to the rest of the faculty. A meaningful program cannot be established without their support. Attend at least some of the faculty meetings—even if you are only a part-time instructor. Get to know the other teachers on a friendship basis. Knowing their instructional objectives, the various units they are studying, and their insights into the children can only reinforce your integration of music education into the total learning experience of the child.

Since the goals of a fulfilling children's music program are interwoven with the child's spiritual development, it is desirable to have close communication with the Christian education director or church school superintendent. This relationship can also create a strong support system with church school teachers and children's workers. It takes teamwork to provide children with an integrated learning environment. Alignment of purpose and mutual support can nurture a healthy program. Fragmentation and isolation can only defeat the cause.

Each organization also needs to consider the positions of accompanist (unless the director serves as his own) and assistants. Much of the musical success of the children's choir will be directly related to the accompanist. He or she must be accurate in note reading/playing and rhythm reading/playing skills. Accompanists who do not read music but simply improvise by ear will be confined to their own style of playing and unable to provide the flexibility and accuracy that comprehensive music education demands. Their sensitivity to the children's accompaniment needs is essential. They must provide adequate support without playing heavily so the children can sing in a confident but non-forceful manner and yet be heard clearly by the audience. A good accompanist will follow the director closely—following tempo, dynamics, and interpretation. Phrasing and characteristics of style need especially to be observed closely.

PERSONNEL—PARENTS

Parent participation and support is also key to operating and organizing a successful program. Many times we have unknowingly created apathy on the part of our parents by letting them feel that we can provide excellent programs for their children. As a result, many congregations and academic communities expect the directors and teachers to do everything, and little volunteer cooperation can be found. For those of us involved in educational programs for the child—especially those that contribute to spiritual development—we need to keep three basic axioms in mind.

First, parents need to participate because it is a fulfillment of their God-given responsibility. The church was not designed by God as the primary agency for Christian education—the home was! The role of the church is to serve as stimulus and resource center to equip homes to do their job better. Deuteronomy 6:7 states: "And you shall teach them diligently to your sons and shall talk of them when you sit in your house and when you walk by the way and when you lie down and when you rise up." We simply are not doing our homes, our children, or our programs justice if we do not require parent involvement. For church programs that enlist children whose parents are not from their church family, we give a hearty congratulation! Perhaps initially you cannot secure the participation of the child's parent—but do not negate the principle. Assign a surrogate parent. Have the parent who brings the child, or the mother of the child with whom the youngster attends fill the gap of the "responsible parent" until such time as the child's parents are willing to fulfill their own responsibility.

Second, parents need to participate because their children need it. Anyone who has been involved in education in any form will recognize that the most influential power on the child's ability to learn—either in a positive or negative way—is his home. Slow learners who have parents who will help them, show interest, and create situations where they can be successful not only increase the success of their present learning but to a large extent determine the success with which they will continue to learn. Conversely, many bright children who come from homes where sincere motivation and communication are missing frequently never reach their potential. An interested parent is a key factor in the child's development—both musically and spiritually.

Third, parents need to participate because the director

needs it. Regardless of the talents of a gifted children's music director, there simply are not enough hours or enough hands to do the work that a comprehensive program requires. Directors who get bogged down with having to keep attendance records, filing and distributing music, lining up transportation, designing staging and scenery, placing microphones, etc., will have the ultimate purpose of their ministry severely curtailed. It is not humanly possible to care for all these details—all vitally important—and minister to the children on a meaningful personal level. A good parent organization can solve these operational complexities. Remember in Exodus 17, Moses sent Joshua out to war with the Amalekites and promised to go to the top of the mountain and pray. Recall that as long as Moses held up his hands the Israelites were winning, but when he let down his hands the Amalekites prevailed. "But Moses' hands were heavy. Then they took a stone and put it under him, and he sat on it; and Aaron and Hur supported his hands, one on one side and one on the other. Thus his hands were steady until the sun set" (Ex. 17:12). Regardless of God's divine appointment and Moses' tremendous leadership, he was unable to do the job without others holding up his hands. The success of a leader is in direct proportion to the support system sustaining his ministry.

Once we recognize that parents need to be involved for their own benefit, their child's benefit, and the director's benefit, we are faced with the problem of how to organize an effective parents' program. One way is by beginning the year with a parents' reception or orientation meeting. This meeting should be a required part of the enrollment process. Those unable to attend should be required to have a personal interview with the director to go over the information. Those in Christian schools can simply present their program as part of the overall curriculum—either at an open house or parents' night. Membership in choir—although open to all children—should be by registration only. This insures that all children and parents will have to go through proper enrollment procedures—including enlistment of the parent in the parents' guild.

Specific communication and retention will be best achieved if the parents have some kind of handout or booklet to take home with them. This will give them opportunity to review the program once they have gone home—share it with others—and review the policies during the year. Booklets do not need to be elaborate, but they do need to contain all essential elements of your program. Usually these elements fall into five categories:

1. Purpose: Let them know your purpose in terms of both music education and Christian education. Let them know your desire to develop some performance skills and establish a responsible ministry. It helps parents and directors alike when their purpose is not nebulous, but clearly spelled out in writing for all to see.

2. Program: Show them the curriculum. Share how specific instructional objectives will help you achieve your purpose. Let them go through some of the materials with you. This is an excellent opportunity for them to purchase their own child's materials—especially if you use consumable student materials—the superior way to function. It will assure their continued interest if it has involved their pocketbook—regardless of the amount.

3. Performances: Communicating dates, time, and location of all programs and dress rehearsals will avoid countless scheduling conflicts later in the year. Also, be sure to outline appropriate wardrobe for each performance. Specify whether the children will be wearing choir robes, coordinated outfits, costumes, or something that needs to be purchased in advance. Don't risk inappropriate attire by waiting to send notes home later in the year with wardrobe instructions.

4. Policy: Specify all regulations and resulting consequences. Any worthwhile program will have policies governing attendance, tardiness, dress rehearsals, and possibly a reward system. Patterns of unfaithfulness and tardiness are established in childhood. Many directors bemoan the lack of commitment of their children or parents or both, but do nothing to make this lack of discipline meet with consequences. Establishing guidelines in advance will avoid reinforcing patterns unsuitable for ministry.

5. Participation: Present the various opportunities for involvement. Have a variety of suggestions—some suited for parents who have little or "no" time, others suited for those

who would like more involvement. Regardless of a parent's availability, he should be required to sign up for at least one area of involvement. Phoning—for recruitment, absentee follow-up, or program details; wardrobe maintenance—costume construction or choir robe ironing and repair; transportation; staging—design, construction, and set-up; lighting; publicity—design and distribution; performance chaperones; refreshments for special occasions; rehearsal assistants—records, librarian, and aides—all are possible areas of involvement.

Once parents have registered their children and enlisted in their supportive responsibility, use them. Be sure to call on them for the area in which they have agreed to help. Even though their involvement may be minimal, you will accomplish more by using them than by neglecting them. And as your program grows and they work with you year after year, you will begin to develop a loyalty to the program that otherwise may never have matured.

PERSONNEL—CHILDREN

Without children we have no program at all! If you are in a school situation, recruitment for classroom music is not a consideration—you have a captive audience. But recruitment for your select chorus is a factor. And in the church ministry, recruitment is a must.

Starting a program requires energy, enthusiasm, and visibility. Once the program is off to a good start, recruitment becomes more of an outgrowth. To start a program you should have public announcements and endorsements from the senior pastor and all pastoral staff. The board and music committee should participate in publicizing the program and help in recruitment. Posters, buttons, special invitations, newsletters, bulletins, and flyers are only a few suggestions for publicizing your program. Use bulletin boards. Initiate phone-a-thons. Visit Sunday school classes. In short, go wherever there are children or parents. Talk to them. Enthusiasm is contagious! Get it spreading for you!

Age-grouping must be considered. Classification of children into specific choirs will, in part, be determined by the circumstances of individual situations. General groupings would be:

Early-childhood choir—preschool and kindergarten children.
Primary choir—ages six, seven, and eight (grades 1-3)
Junior choir—ages nine to twelve (grades 4-6)

Sometimes large churches are able to offer a more highly graded program, such as a choir for every two grades or even a choir for each grade. If you have enough children and competent leadership to staff this kind of a program, it can work well. Just remember that to divide the children into too small groups will diminish peer and group momentum. Also, a highly graded situation necessitates more competent staff. It is better to arrange the children into larger groups with good leadership than assign directors who are not capable of handling the demands of children's music leadership. Communication and coordination of goals, materials, and programs also becomes more challenging with highly graded situations.

There are corresponding pitfalls in assigning too many children to one choir—lack of personal attention and motivation, for instance. The individual situation should determine the organization. The children are the reason for the program. Their needs should be taken into consideration. Corralling them like a herd or isolating them from meaningful interaction can devastate a choir program. It may be best to start with the recommended divisions, and then further subdivide as the need becomes evident.

As far as what the children can achieve—don't underestimate their abilities. The limitations frequently placed on children's musical competence have been much more a reflection of the director's capabilities than true evaluations of the children's ability. Children are capable of a great deal musically. The key is in teaching the way they learn, and sequencing their activities properly. When these principles are followed, we frequently find their accomplishments will surprise us.

FACILITY AND EQUIPMENT

It is difficult to encourage children to sing if the room is dismal and damp. Rooms need to be large (public education requires a minimum of thirty-five square feet per child), well lighted, and well ventilated. Paint and windows should be

174

kept clean. Walls should have appropriate posters, bulletin boards, and charts. Remember to keep all wall decorations at the eye-level of the children.

Furniture needs to be suitable for the child's age. It is difficult to conduct an early-childhood choir if the children are sitting in adult folding chairs. The children seem to constantly be sliding through the opening in the back or pinching themselves in the hinges or trying to get their feet to touch the floor. When possible, it is nice to have the room divided into three areas—one for singing (with appropriate size chairs), one for movement (with no furniture at all, but a carpet if possible), and one for writing (with tables and chairs). The following floor plans are examples of these suggestions:

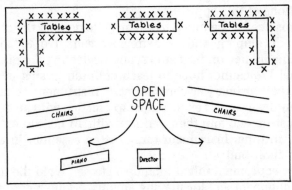

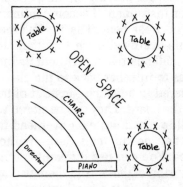

When rooms do not allow this much space, arrange for the children to do their writing activities at their chairs. This can be accomplished by using the chairs that have extended writing arms. If this is not possible, you can provide clipboards for the children to store under their chairs and use for writing. If it is impossible to have a separate open space for movement activities, be sure to place the chairs (or desks) far enough apart that the children will have ample room to move standing by their seats. This, however, is the least desirable condition. It is difficult to maintain a child's interest for an entire hour when he is confined to one location. In addition, sitting at desks or in rows of chairs is not conducive to involving the child in psychomotor experiences—an essential in learning. Much of this limitation of space has prompted our children's music programs to be handled the same way as adult music programs—mostly focused on "sitting still and singing"—and we have established the severe limitations of this approach.

Pianos need to be tuned frequently! Remember the child's ear is developing and is extremely sensitive to sound. Spending money on furnishings and neglecting the piano is a crime! We cannot hope to teach children to sing in tune when their primary accompaniment instrument is out of tune. And we cannot expect them to practice with an out-of-tune instrument, and then perform with an instrument that is kept in tune. Instrument tuning is an essential in every graded choir budget.

Other equipment might include a stereo (avoid the use of "toy" phonographs) for playing albums, a tape recorder for using cassettes or instrumental accompaniment, rhythm instruments, and of great benefit is the overhead projector. Teaching with the overhead projector offers the same benefits as using the chalkboard—but without its limitations. The teacher never has to turn her back to the class. Transparencies can be prepared in advance—instead of taking up class time to write on the board. They can be stored without fear of erasure. The children can write on overhead transparencies the same way they do on their desk—without having to stretch on tiptoes. You can use different colors to create interest or note division of parts. And there is none of the mess of chalkdust. All in all, it is a good way to teach.

A director ought to have a podium or music stand for her music—although most of the music should be memorized before attempting to teach it to the children. Use of music in rehearsal should be for referral purposes only. Also, lesson plans and teaching aids can be placed on the podium or director's desk.

Keep in mind what is essential and what is optional. Rhythm instruments for each child do not need to be purchased immediately—or all at once. Each child can use his own body percussions. Then rhythm instruments can be added as there is available budget to procure good ones.

Some teachers use guitar or autoharp. These are fine instruments for accompaniment variety but do not offer the flexibility of keyboard accompaniment. Others teach the children to sing *a cappella*—without accompaniment. This method is excellent—as long as the instructor exhibits good vocal production and quality.

Children's music books are essential. Rote instruction is fine occasionally, but should be avoided as a perpetual habit in teaching technique. Individual student books increase motivation and retention.

Select your room. Determine its needs. Tune your piano. Itemize your materials and equipment in order of priority. Prepare a comprehensive budget. If finances are inadequate, try a fund-raising project. Involve the children and parents. Don't be frustrated over what you don't have. Build a quality program, and the rest will come in time.

CURRICULUM AND MATERIALS

Because we have established the fact that *curriculum* is a broad term, and have suggested that many music materials are more correctly identified as "materials" rather than curriculum, we have prepared the following list as a composite of several types of materials. *Curriculum* is a specific, highly technical term that includes statement of purpose, specific instructional objectives, properly selected content, properly sequenced activities, and evaluative or feedback techniques. *Music Is for Children,* published by David C. Cook, represents this kind of comprehensive curriculum. If the materials you select do not incorporate all these ingredients, you will have to fill in the gaps on your own.

Music Publishers

Abingdon Press
201 Eighth Ave. S.
Nashville, TN 37202

A.M.S.I.
Minneapolis, MN 55408

Augsburg Publishing House
426 South 5th Street
Minneapolis, MN 55415

Beckenhorst Press
P.O. Box 14273
Columbus, OH 43214

Belwin-Mills Publishing Corp.
Melville, NY 11746

Benson Publishing Co.
1625 Broadway
Nashville, TN 37202

Birdwing Music
8587 Canoga Avenue
Canoga Park, CA 91304

Bock, Fred, Music Co.
Box 333
Tarzana, CA 91356

Boosey and Hawkes
Oceanside, NY 11572

Boston Music Co.
116 Boylston St.
Boston, MA 02116

Bourne, Inc.
136 W. 52nd St.
New York, NY 10019

Broadman Press
127 N. 9th Ave.
Nashville, TN 37203

Broude, Alexander, Inc.
225 W. 57th St.
New York, NY 10019

Choristers Guild
P.O. Box 38188
Dallas, TX 75238

Concordia Publishing House
3558 S. Jefferson Ave.
St. Louis, MO 63118

Fischer, Carl, Inc.
56-62 Cooper Sq.
New York, NY 10003

Flammer, Harold, Inc.
Delaware Water Gap, PA 18327

Gaither Music
P.O. Box 300
Alexandria, IN 46001

Gentry Publications
P.O. Box 333
Tarzana, CA 91356

Good Life Productions
7901 E. Pierce St.
Scottsdale, AZ 85257

Hinshaw Music, Inc.
P. O. Box 470
Chapel Hill, NC 27514

Hope Publishing Co.
Carol Stream, IL 60187

Jenson Publications, Inc.
2880 So. 171st Street
New Berlin, WI 53151

Leonard, Hal, Publishing Corp.
Winona, MN 55987

Lexicon Music
P. O. Box 296
Woodland Hills, CA 91364

Lillenas Publishing Co.
Kansas City, MO 64141

Lorenz Publishing Co.
510 E. Third St.
Dayton, OH 45401

Manna Music, Inc.
2111 Kenmere Ave.
Burbank, CA

McAfee Music Corp.
300 East 5th St.
New York, NY 10022

Paragon Associates, Inc.
803 Eighteenth Ave. South
Nashville, TN 37202

Presser, Theodore, Co.
Bryn Mawr, PA 19010

Plymouth Music Co., Inc.
17 West 60th St.
New York, NY 10023

Proclamation Productions Inc.
Orange Square
Port Jervis, NY 12771

178

Richmond Music Press, Inc.
P. O. Box 465
Richmond, IN 47374

Schirmer, E. C.
112 South St.
Boston, MA 02111

Schirmer, G.
609 Fifth Ave.
New York, NY 10017

Shawnee Press, Inc.
Delaware Water Gap, PA 18327

Singspiration, Inc.
1415 Lake Dr. S.E.
Grand Rapids, MI 49506

Triune Music, Inc.
824 19th Ave. South
Box 23088
Nashville, TN 37202

Volkwein Brothers, Inc.
117 Sandusky St.
Pittsburgh, PA 15212

Willis Music Co.
440 Main St.
Cincinnati, OH 45202

Word, Inc.
Waco, TX 76703

Zondervan Publishing House
1415 Lake Drive, S.E.
Grand Rapids, MI 49506

Curriculum Materials

David C. Cook Publishing
850 North Grove Ave.
Elgin, IL 60120

MUSIC IS FOR CHILDREN

Choristers Guild
P. O. Box 38188
Dallas, TX 75238

THE NOTES OF MUSIC

Fortress Press
Philadelphia, PA 19129

CHILDREN SING

Carl Fischer
62 Cooper Square
New York, NY 10003

MY FAVORITE HYMNS OF
PRAISE (and others by Mabel S.
Boyter)

Praise Hymn, Inc.
P. O. Box 401767
Garland, TX 75040

GOD MADE MUSIC (series)

Broadman Press
127 N. 9th Ave.
Nashville, TN 37203

MELODY MAKERS & MUSIC
MAKERS

Shawnee Press
Delaware Water Gap, PA 18327

THE SIGHT AND SOUND OF
MUSIC

Augsburg Publishing House
426 S. 5th St.
Minneapolis, MN 55415

ALLELUIA

Magazines and Publications

CREATOR
5901 E. Crater Lake Ave.
Orange, CA 92667

JOURNAL OF CHURCH MUSIC
2900 Queen Lane
Philadelphia, PA 19129

THE CHORAL JOURNAL
THE HYMN
The Hymn Society of America
Wittenberg University
Springfield, OH 45501

MUSIC EDUCATORS JOURNAL
Music Educators National Conference
1201 16th St. N.W.
Washington, DC 20036

Professional Organizations

The Hymn Society of America
Wittenberg University
Springfield, OH 45501

National Church Music Fellowship
% Dr. William Tromble
Houghton College
Houghton, NY 14744

American Guild of Organists
630 Fifth Avenue
New York, NY 10020

Music Educators National Conference
1201 16th St. N.W.
Washington, DC 20036

American Choral Directors Assn.
1103 C Ave. Suite 7
Lawton, OK 73601

Children's Hymnals

Hymns for the Children of God
Paragon (1981)

Joyful Sounds
Concordia (1977)

Junior Hymnal
Broadman (1964)

Young Voices in Praise
Benson (1979)

Hymns for Junior Worship
Westminster Press (1946)

Hymns for Primary Worship
Westminster Press (1946)

10
Music in the
Christian School

Today's Christian school movement is an effort on the part of
Bible believers to provide an educational program in which
Christ is honored and the teachings of God's Word are freely
shared.
Dr. Paul Kienel

CHRISTIAN SCHOOLS HAVE ENJOYED phenomenal growth
rates in the last decade. Predominant in their purpose is the
determination to teach all academic subjects within the perspective of Scripture. They focus all curriculum from this
viewpoint.

MUSIC IN THE CURRICULUM
Music is essential in the child's development of his world
view—in relationship to himself, to God, and to his world.
We have examined the role that music plays in the development of pure cognitive skills. It is beneficial in perceptual
development. It aids in learning to read. It amplifies math
skills. It is significant in affective development. It develops
self-esteem. It develops aesthetic understanding and communicates *to* and *from* the emotions. It develops peer relationships through teamwork and ensemble participation. It
develops psychomotor skills—listening skills, fine-motor
coordination, and writing skills. It fosters creativity. Music
is beneficial in religious cognitive skills. It aids in the internalization of doctrine. It facilitates Scripture memorization.
It builds biblical vocabulary. Music is critical in the child's
spiritual affective development. It aids in building Christian

character. It reflects biblical values—and can significantly affect the development of the child's attitudes. It communicates God's unconditional love. And music is valuable in the development of biblically oriented psychomotor skills—communicating truth, sharing God's love, and relating personal experiences. The culmination of this kind of learning will substantially influence the child's world view.

Quality music education should also serve to develop the child's relationship to God—another stated distinctive of the Christian school movement. Many Christian schools provide chapel times for their students. Some of these gatherings focus on worship. We noted in the first section of this book that music has been an integral part of worship since the days of the Old Testament. In fact, singing to the Lord was not an option, but a law (see Ps. 81:1-4). If we wish to instill the fact that worship is not a spectator sport but an active function of individuals and groups praising God, then we must involve them in worship during childhood. Music is a most natural expression to God.

Music is significant in corporate edification—another purpose for chapel services in the Christian school. Reaffirming biblical truths as a group lets the children feel the community of the Body of Christ. Schools that do not provide music education in the curriculum but attempt to use it in any dimension during chapel are frequently victims of their own neglect. If music is a medium of expression worthy of God's audience, then it certainly is worthy of inclusion in our curriculum. The existence of a gap between the music in our curriculum (either its nonexistence, or its totally different substance) says one thing: Either the music we sing in the class is not suitable for God, or the music we sing in chapel is not suitable for class. What a tragic dichotomy!

If music is a valid expression of worship—and it is—then Christian music deserves attention in education—it is worth learning! This kind of music instruction will significantly affect the development of the child's relationship to God. This does not mean that we should never do anything but religious music in Christian schools. Many secular songs are part of our American heritage. Many nonreligious songs teach good values. This is, rather, a statement of where our primary focus belongs.

Music not only helps the child understand who he is and who God is, but who others are—both within the family of God and the world at large. Educating the whole child calls for development of this perspective. We do not engage in the instruction of academic subjects just so a child can successfully perform in the classroom. We must equip the child so he can perform in life! A comprehensive music education program gives a child a gift for life. If developed properly it will not end the day he receives his diploma, but will continue to provide a means of relating to his world. Because music breaks down many barriers between peoples, those who have had their lives enriched through its meaning can pass it on. Music reflects different cultures. It can help the student expand his cultural appreciation—social studies at its best. It can provide substance for his own creative expression—speech in its most powerful form. It can help him relate in a secure, non-threatening manner to his peers and superiors—the culmination of psychology. And it places within the human person the innate ability to understand form and meaning—science personified. Music belongs at the core of our curriculum.

But we must be quick to recognize that simply the inclusion of music in the curriculum does not insure these benefits. Music has been in public education for many years and has never succeeded in fulfilling all its potential. We must honestly face this realization. The principal weakening factor in public music education, according to Thomas Regelski, whose research is contained in his *Principles and Problems of Music Education*, is that the primary focus of too much music education has been performance, rather than on developing musical individuals. This is exemplified by the marching band, festival choirs, etc. The problem with this approach is: What do you do with it after graduation? Elementary music focuses on musical facts rather than involving the child in meaningful musical expressions and developing his own creativity. Until musical facts are integrated into meaningful personal expression, they remain another academic activity—whether in public or Christian school. What Regelski is saying is that for music education to be meaningful, it must be comprehensive. It cannot be simply a cognitive skill of memorizing musical taxonomies, or a psychomotor skill of polished performance. It must involve the total child, including the affective domain—value and character considerations, creative and cohesive skills.

The problem is that the determining values in public education are humanistic and secularistic in foundation. Music that reflects these values can be as damaging as other academic disciplines that are taught from this perspective. This is where the Christian school can make a difference. Because it is taught from the biblical perspective, music education has a potential in the Christian school that it does not have anywhere else. It has the opportunity to reach the whole person. It has the opportunity to affect culture. Christian school music curriculum should no more be a transplant of public music education than any other discipline—in fact, even less so. Because music involves all three domains of learning—cognitive, affective, and psychomotor—learning through music is more efficient and retention is greater.

We must perceive our distinctives clearly—one of substance, the other of approach and focus. We simply cannot put all our efforts into developing fine musical performing groups at the expense of neglecting comprehensive music education for the whole child. While it is true that music groups can provide added exposure for the Christian school by performing for civic organizations and supporting churches, and while it is true that school-sponsored groups are excellent means of outreach (all valid areas of musical development), they should never be perceived to be the substance of our music program. A comprehensive music program will provide both. The performance will be the result, not the reason for being. Incorporating comprehensive music education in early-childhood and elementary curriculum will inevitably elevate performance levels. Many high school choirs are filled with students who are musically illiterate. This tragedy not only limits them to rote instruction—so they can perform—but prevents any further development. This is not music education, but music exploitation.

MUSIC IN THE CLASSROOM
Music should be scheduled for a minimum of one hour per

week—either all at once or divided into two half-hour sessions. It is almost impossible to accomplish anything significant in any less time. Before seasonal performances such as at Christmas, the time allotment should be increased.

Student materials should be purchased by the parents. This should not be a cause for embarrassment for the school. Much public education is either eliminating many of the quality student materials, which undercuts the program, or requiring parents to purchase these supplies. Children's music materials for the year will be more than covered by a charge of $1.00 per month. When parents are convinced of the worth of the program, they will gladly provide for necessary materials. Most parents want music education for their children.

Another way to build parent support is to get parents involved. During the course of the year, let each class develop its own music project—maybe putting together a program for the retirement home in the community, perhaps featuring some original compositions by the children; or put together a program of creative musical expressions for the local cable TV station; or perform Christmas carols at the shopping center; or hold a special parents' night music reception, featuring some singing, rhythmic expressions, and creative compositions. Get parents to assist. Use the same principles that were presented in chapter 9.

Engage the children in fund-raising projects to cover budget deficiencies. Jog-a-thons, calendar sales, bake sales—the list of possibilities is limitless—all can help the music budget. Parents are more than happy to support meaningful educational curriculum for their children, and community businessmen frequently consider it their civic responsibility to sponsor worthwhile causes. Whatever the need, think creatively to solve it. Classroom music is the substance of your program and the foundation of your musical future.

11
Conducting an Effective Rehearsal

While choral singing reaches the audience or congregation in the public performance, it is, in reality, in the regular rehearsal that the choral experience finds its true identity; put more simply, the location of the choral experience is the rehearsal.

Ray Robinson

RUNNING A GOOD REHEARSAL takes more than good materials. It is the rehearsal that transforms the material into *experience*. Objectives, while vitally important, exist on paper—rehearsals exist in people. We cannot have inferior rehearsals—run carelessly by "the seat of the pants"—and consider our ministry satisfactory based on acceptable performances. For as Dr. Robinson states, "The location of the choir experience is the rehearsal." It is the week-by-week rehearsal that will have an indelible effect on the child—his attitudes toward music, ministry, choir, leadership, and much more—long after he is grown. We cannot regard the rehearsal only as a means to an end. It is an end in itself. A good director will take both aspects into consideration.

REHEARSAL PREPARATION
The success of a rehearsal is born in the preparation of the director. Preparation is a many-faceted responsibility. We examined the concerns of readiness, motivation, and retention in chapter 5. We established the need for instructional objectives in chapter 7, and the "experience" approach to learning in chapter 8. But preparation includes more than this.

A good director needs to prepare musically. This means he must carefully learn the music prior to presenting it to the children. He should know the various parts—melody, rhythm, and text. He needs to know the personality of the music—proper tempo, dynamics, phrasing, and interpretative techniques such as staccato, legato, marcato, or dolce. He needs to know what teaching techniques he will use for various parts of the song. How will he teach the children the words, melody, or rhythm? What tempo will he use to teach the music? Is it the same tempo he will use in performance? Music preparation includes rehearsing with the accompanist. Any differences in interpretation, or musical mistakes need to be worked out privately before rehearsing with the children.

A good director needs to prepare his materials. This includes the preparation of teaching aids and student materials. Neglecting this will almost invariably cause embarrassment sometime during the rehearsal. Even the use of ready-made teaching aids requires some preparation on the part of the director. Sometimes they need to be cut out from a large chart, or laminated with clear adhesive paper. Sometimes overhead transparencies or certain flashcards need to be selected and put aside for rehearsal use. Adequate supplies of pencils, paper, and student books need to be counted out carefully. Equipment needs to be requisitioned and room arrangement taken care of. Know ahead of time where you are going to place the overhead projector, stereo, or tape recorder.

A good director needs to prepare spiritually. Ministry requires the posture of humility and servanthood. Neither are possible without prayer and Bible study. The challenge of children's character and attitude development demands that our deportment and attitudes are exemplary of the biblical pattern. Pray as a team—director and accompanist. Pray as a staff—ministerial, musical, and children's department. As Tennyson wrote, "More things are wrought by prayer than this world dreams of." Don't let the urgent squeeze out the vital. A fulfilling children's music ministry demands prayer!

A good director needs to prepare physically. Next to one's own self-image, the persons most affected by the director's appearance are the children. Sloppy attire communicates a lack of worth. Dress neatly and select pleasing colors. Children notice colors. Adequate sleep is a prerequisite for the patience you will need. Good health is necessary to fulfill your commitment. Physical preparation gets the person inside the director ready to face the children.

Finally, prepare logistically! Arrive at rehearsal early. If the children arrive at rehearsal before the director, he is entering "their" territory. If the director arrives before the children, they are entering "his" territory—a fine line of distinction but critical to the establishment of good discipline. Early arrival gives you time to make sure your room is ready—chairs in the right places, tables where they belong, equipment working—take time to turn on the overhead projector. If the bulb is burned out, you ought to know it *before* the children arrive. Arrange your teaching aids so they will be easily accessible—in the proper sequence. Have your assistant or volunteer parent ready with attendance records. If it is your first rehearsal, have name tags ready. Begin from the first moment to call children by their name. Pointing to the child "in the third row with the gray slacks" is strictly taboo. Finally, greet the children at the door—individually if possible. They should feel that you are prepared for them personally and ready for the rehearsal musically.

REHEARSAL CONTENT

All experiences need to focus around the instructional objective for the lesson, but there are additional considerations in organizing rehearsal content.

First, children learn in short attention spans. Once children enter school, their attention span increases, but children usually do not concentrate steadily for long periods of time. We cannot design our rehearsal around the few who are able to handle lengthy concentration, because it only takes one or two children to break the momentum of the class time. We cannot face an hour with a list of three or four things we want to cover, and then "play it by ear." For not only do children learn in short spans, the most aggressive period of their learning is at the beginning of their concentration. Their time of aggressive learning peaks very quickly and then levels off and gradually diminishes. If we prolong our activities, we are always passing their best learning stage and catching them somewhere on the downhill side. If we go too far we fight boredom and discipline problems. Activities for preschool choir should not exceed three to four minutes at the beginning of the year. Depending on the group, this may be lengthened to a maximum of five to six minutes by the end of the year. Primary choir activities should average seven minutes and gradually build up to ten minutes. Junior choir members can usually concentrate on one activity for eight to fifteen minutes, depending on the nature of the experience. These are not hard and fast rules but general guidelines.

This means that if we are facing music rehearsal for one hour a week, we need to have specifically designed:

- at least twenty activities for pre-schoolers;
- at least eight to nine activities for primaries;
- at least six to eight activities for juniors.

While this may initially seem a gargantuan job, if we take time to list the various ingredients that are *essential* in a comprehensive music program, we find out just how limited we are. One hour is really too short! There are so many exciting elements of music education that one cannot possibly cover each element every week. This is all the more reason for making careful rehearsal plans—you can plan your rehearsals to complement one another. What you don't cover one week, you can cover the next. In so doing, each unit (or approximately one month's work) will fit cohesively together to form a whole. This way, you can also keep track of activities that were completed successfully and ones that need additional reinforcement.

Essential elements are:

Music Fundamentals
   Rhythm
      1. experiencing rhythm
      2. expanding rhythmic experience through variety
      3. visualization of rhythm experience
      4. visualization with experience
      5. reinforcement of rhythm experience through expansion and creativity (transfer)
      6. writing rhythm experience
      7. composing a rhythm expression (transfer)

189

Staff reading
1. experiencing "on a line" and "in a space"
2. expanding staff reading experience
3. visualization of staff experience
4. visualization with experience
5. reinforcement through expansion (transfer)
6. writing notes "on lines"and "in spaces"
7. learning musical alphabet—forwards (up) and backwards (down)
8. placing musical alphabet on staff
9. singing melodic patterns by note name
10. selecting melodic patterns to create phrases
11. composing melodic patterns to complete phrases (transfer)

Repertoire Singing
1. experiencing a unison
2. expanding melodic imitation
3. participating in vocal exercises
   a. developing breath support
   b. maintaining good posture
   c. developing good articulation
   d. experiencing resonation
4. singing by note name
5. learning new songs
   a. imitative singing
   b. note-name singing
   c. singing individual phrases
6. learning new texts
7. performing repertoire

Scriptural Fundamentals
Internalization of central theme
1. Establishment of scriptural focus through dialogue
2. Discussion of scriptural theme—expansion
3. Personal expression of scriptural theme

Scripture memorization
1. Relationship to central theme
2. Learning the Scripture verses
3. Relating the Scripture verses to the child's life
4. Participating in memory and reinforcement activities
5. Creative expression of verse or scriptural content.

Thus we see at least thirty-three different types of activities that need to be incorporated into our program. The three basic categories—music fundamentals, repertoire singing, and Scripture instruction—need to be the skeletal structure for each rehearsal. To this skeleton we need to add the "meat" of each class or rehearsal time. It is essential to note the sequential build-up of the music experiences. The rhythm ♩ ♩ ♩ 𝄾 cannot be considered really learned until it has been experienced, expanded, visualized, reinforced, written, and transferred to creative expression.

These elements need not all be in the same lesson plan. Perhaps one week the children will experience ♩ ♩ ♩ 𝄾 by clapping and expand it to snapping or rhythm instruments. Then the next week they may add the visualization aspect and experience the rhythm with visualization. Expansion and reinforcement activities may spread over the next few weeks or be condensed to another lesson. Writing can be incorporated rather quickly or delayed accordingly. Since it is the writing that combines the experience, visual discrimination, and makes it a personal expression, it is wisest not to delay it too long. If a child has experienced quarter notes, visualized quarter notes, read quarter notes from the page or visual aid, combined his visualization with experience, he can write quarter notes! Integration into the individual, which is exhibited through creative expression, then becomes a possibility. The same principle holds true for staff reading. We do not need to cover each item in each rehearsal, but our activities need to represent a properly sequenced organization of material.

Our repertoire singing needs to provide time for vocal warm-up, review of a familiar song, reinforcement of repertoire that is being learned, and exposure to future repertoire. This principle, coupled with the biblical pattern of variety of type (psalms, hymns, and spiritual songs), will prevent our getting into musical ruts. To spend an entire year learning one or two musicals is tragic—for two reasons: First, it is far below the child's capability to learn new music; second, it does not follow a biblical balance of type. Much children's repertoire is run dry with repetition before it is filed away. How unfortunate to destroy the impact of good repertoire by overexposure.

Scriptural focus should be part of each rehearsal. It should follow different formats. One week can be the illustration of a Bible narrative, the next a dialogue of questions and answers, the following a time of dialogue with personal expression. It should all be substantiated through Scripture memorization. Remember, personal interpretation is only valid as long as it lines up with scriptural statement.

Choir members should feel they are integral members of the Body of Christ. Take time to share needs, show Christian concern, and pray together. It is not enough to wish good luck or say "God bless us." This is a ministry! It needs to be watered with prayer.

Once you have your skeletal structure dressed with the appropriate activities, decide on time allocation for each item. This will keep your rehearsal moving. Sometimes problems arise when you get involved in an activity, and you forget that you need to keep moving. Momentum can die easily, and once gone, it is difficult to restore. You might want to plan an alternate activity or two in case one that you had planned doesn't work for any variety of reasons. Then write out carefully your plan. Initially it may be complex, but as you get into the habit, you will learn how to abbreviate. Keep it workable. One sample would be:

Instructional objectives:

1. Given the rhythm ♩ ♩ | ♩. | ♩ ♩ ♩ | ♩. (which is the rhythm from their repertoire selection "Be My Lord"), the children will experience the rhythm by direct imitation, using a clap, snap, patchen, and stomp. They will expand this experience by dividing the class into four groups, altering the patterns, and performing them on various rhythm instruments.

2. Given the song "Be My Lord," the children will develop their sight-singing ability by first identifying the notes of the melody by name, and then singing them by name.

3. The children will begin learning "Lord, I Want to Be a Christian" by listening to the song sung, and following along in their student books. This theme will be correlated with Joshua 24:24 later in the lesson by giving the children opportunity to share ways of serving the Lord.

4. Given specific notes on the staff, the children will review staff reading by naming two notes in each example, and then count the distance between the first and second note to identify the interval.

5. Given the notes on the grand staff (with the exception of bass B-A-G) the students will review the notes by naming them when called on. They will then be introduced to bass B-A-G, and will be asked to identify them when written on the transparency for the overhead projector and visualized on a flashcard.

Once the teacher has itemized these clearly stated instructional objectives, he may choose to abbreviate somewhat (see "General Objectives" in lesson plan below). Then outline specific materials needed and list them at the top of your plan (see "Preparation" section in lesson plan that follows). Finally, design carefully the activities that will achieve each of these objectives.

REHEARSAL EVALUATION

Be sure to keep either a good notebook or notes in the margins of your lesson plans. Note activities that were eliminated because of time limitation. Note activities that seemed difficult for the children. Although you might not repeat them the next week (and sometimes you shouldn't) you will want to observe patterns of the class. Are there types of activities that always seem difficult? When we recognize patterns forming, we may need to adjust our approach.

A good music curriculum will not be linear in progression, but *spiral* in development. It does not assume that the children will master each activity the first time. It also recognizes that each child learns differently. Based on these two facts, the same material will be recycled again at some future point, perhaps in a little different way with a slightly adjusted focus. It is better to keep moving, keep evaluating, and when a pattern becomes consistent, make adjustments, expansions, or alterations. When a child senses that a teacher is frustrated (and indeed they are very perceptive), it causes two things: It causes them to be frustrated with themselves, a reflection of the teacher's attitude; and it causes insecurity by emphasizing the failure, what the child *can't* do, instead of what he *can* do.

Evaluation by the students is also important. They need to have visible indications of progress and accomplishment. Performances only evaluate one thing—their ability to per-

UNIT 5

GENERAL OBJECTIVES

Students will:

- learn the rhythm to "Be My Lord" and note-read the melody.
- learn "Lord, I Want to Be a Christian" and Joshua 24: 24.
- identify intervals.
- review the notes they know and add the last three notes of the bass staff, B-A-G.

PREPARATION

Supplies: Overhead projector (or chalkboard)

Transparency 18

Rhythm instruments—rhythm sticks, claves, clappers, wood blocks, triangles, bells, drums, cymbals, and tambourines—if you have them

Flash cards of the twenty-one notes of the grand staff (one note on each card)

Pencils or crayons

RHYTHM EXPERIENCE (10 minutes)

Students learn the rhythm to "Be My Lord" using rhythm instruments or body motions, and then perform to the piano accompaniment.

Begin today's class by having the children seated in two groups. Ask them to imitate you, and clap ♩ ♩ | ♩ ♪ . ' Use all body motions to perform the same rhythmic pattern. Then tell them you are going to do two patterns together, and clap ♩ ♩ | ♩ ♪ . followed by patchen ♩ ♩ | ♩ ♪ .

Repeat this rhythmic "question and answer" using several different body motions such as ♩ ♩ | ♩ ♪ . (snap), ♩ ♪ . (clap); ♩ ♩ | ♩ ♪ . (stomp), ♩ ♩ | ♩ ♪ . (patchen), etc. You can even vary this with a few body motions of your own, such as tapping your shoulders or touching the end of your ear.

Since the class is already divided into two groups, ask one group to imitate the first part of your pattern and the other to imitate the second. It would be nice to perform the two sections together without the echo. But if the children get confused, do the question first and wait for it to be repeated, then do the answer. Again, repeat this using several different combinations of body motions and switching the groups every few turns.

Finally, pass out rhythm instruments if you have them. Divide the rhythm instruments into four sound families: (1) rhythm sticks, claves, clappers, and wood blocks, (2) triangles and bells, (3) drums and cymbals, (4) tambourines.

78

194

If you don't have rhythm instruments, divide the class into four groups and assign a specific body motion to each group. Then place transparency 18 on the projector, and assign each group to play one line. Go through it completely several times:

(Group 1)

(Group 2)

(Group 3)

(Group 4)

When the children can go through all four lines without stopping, go to the piano and add the piano accompaniment to "Be My Lord." The children will learn the words later; for now, it's enough for them to hear the music overlaid onto their rhythms.

SINGING (7 minutes)
Students begin to learn "Lord, I Want to Be a Christian."

You might begin with a familiar song like "Take My Life and Let It Be." Talk about the responsibility we have to serve the Lord when we are part of his family.

Then have the children turn to page 13, in their books, "Lord, I Want to Be a Christian," and sing this song with you. They may already know it since it is an American folk melody. If they don't, you can sing it for them once while they follow the words.

Introduce all four verses today. Remind the children that this would be a good New Year's resolution. Not only should it be our desire to be like Jesus, but the Bible commands us to be like him.

STAFF READING (8 minutes)
Students identify different intervals.

Now ask the children to look at page 12.

Tell them you want them to count the amount of space between the two notes in number 1. Count C-D-E-F with them, which is a fourth. They should put the number 4 in the blank. Then ask them to fill in the numbers for the rest of the page.

When they have completed their work, ask volunteers to identify each example—first they should give the name of each note and then identify the interval.

SINGING WITH STAFF READING
(5 or 7 minutes)

Students note-read and sing the melody of "Be My Lord."

Ask the children to turn to page 19. Have them put their finger on the number 1, which identifies the first verse. Ask them the name of the first note after 1, which is A. If they give the correct answer, they are probably in the right place.

Now go through the song note by note, and have the children give the names. You might mention the natural sign beside B in the seventh measure. Just tell them that it means to sing regular B instead of B flat, but don't get into a lengthy discussion.

After they have gone through the top part or verse 1, go back and sing the tune by note name with piano accompaniment. Have the

79

- Being kind to other people
"And be ye kind one to another, tenderhearted, forgiving one another, even as God for Christ's sake hath forgiven you." Ephesians 4:32
- Caring for other people's needs
"Bear ye one another's burdens, and so fulfill the law of Christ." Galatians 6:2
- Love one another
"A new commandment I give unto you, That ye love one another; as I have loved you, that ye also love one another." John 13:34
- Obey your parents
"Children, obey your parents in all things: for this is well pleasing unto the Lord." Colossians 3:20

Close this discussion with a time of prayer, asking God to help all of us obey his Word and serve him better.

STAFF READING (8 minutes)
Students identify notes of the grand staff, and then learn the last three notes—low B, A, and G.

Place the **grand staff transparency, number 15,** on the screen. It should have all the notes except bass clef B, A, and G on it. **Point to several notes at random,** and have the children identify them. **Then begin at the top of the treble staff with F and read the notes in descending order.**

When you get to bass clef C, keep on going as if the notes were there. The children will probably continue B-A-G. If not, use the same approach you did in the last unit: What is middle C's neighbor below the line? Who is below clef C? Then who do you think is below bass clef C?

Write B, A, and G on the staff with a transparency pen.
Finally, pass out the twenty-one flash cards that have each note of the grand staff on them. Tell the children you want them to get in order from bass clef G all the way up to treble clef F. Say, "On your mark, get set, go!" and see how quickly they can arrange them-

children follow along, pointing to the notes as they sing. Do this a time or two until they are good at it. You want them to recognize the notes, learn to read music from left to right, and follow along rhythmically—all essential ingredients in learning to read music.

Finally, **go back and sing the words.** (If your class is only thirty minutes, omit this last activity.) Thirty-minute classes end here.

SCRIPTURE INSTRUCTION (12 minutes)
Students sing a melodic rendition of Joshua 24:24, and then share ways to serve the Lord.

After the children put their books away, have them begin snapping a beat. Once they are all with you, begin singing:

The Lord our God will we serve, and his voice will we o-bey.

The Lord our God will we serve, and his voice will we o-bey.

You can sing in a variety of ways—*pianissimo, piano, mezzo forte,* and *forte.* After the children are familiar with it, start around the class, having each child sing it to the next person in "telephone" fashion. After the last person has completed the verse, have them say, "Joshua 24:24" in unison.

Then ask different ones to share ways they can serve the Lord. Be sure to add some of the specific commands listed below:

selves. Once they are in order, have each child hold up his or her card in turn and say the note's name.

WRAP-UP (5 minutes)
Students play an exit-pass game to review Joshua 24:24, "Take My Life and Let It Be," and "Lord, I Want to Be a Christian."

Use the final few minutes of class time for an exit-pass game. The children must give you a New Year's resolution before they can leave—they can quote Joshua 24:24, a verse of "Take My Life and Let It Be," a verse of "Lord, I Want to Be a Christian," or one of the Scriptures that tell how to serve the Lord.

form. Additional evaluation is needed if students are to see the full range of what they have learned. Give them opportunity for written "puzzles" (more commonly referred to as "tests"). These need not be frightening ordeals for the children, but a time when they get to show themselves and the teacher how great they are doing. Again, the teacher needs to be perceptive to patterns of weakness and strength. Did the majority of the class do well or poorly on a specific kind of written response? If so, it is probably a commentary on the approach of the teacher rather than the inability or ability of the class. Children are capable of learning a lot, if we are capable of teaching a lot! Evaluations need to be as comprehensive as the curriculum. When handled properly, this can be a tremendous motivation.

Children also need an opportunity to evaluate verbally. Allow them to share their feelings about repertoire and the various kinds of activities (their most favorite or least favorite). Allowing them to share their evaluations of repertoire doesn't necessarily mean you will do only the things they like. Remember who is the director—your perspective is more mature than theirs. But it does mean that they feel free to respond to the music and communicate that response. Performances should also be evaluated. Let the children express how they feel about their own performance. Then the director can share his or her perspective.

Evaluation should also include the leadership—both those who work with you and those to whom you are responsible. Many times their perspective adds a dimension the director doesn't see. The one rule to remember when leadership is participating in evaluation is: Evaluate according to stated purpose and specific objectives. How well have the specific goals originally set been achieved? To evaluate on any other basis is unfair and irresponsible, and does not relate the evaluation to the educative process. Many times a director can become discouraged with the immediate, while the leadership—not susceptible to the week-by-week reaction of the students—can provide an encouraging word and reinforce how much the director has achieved. Other times leadership may base evaluation on criteria that has not been communicated and irrelevant areas may be brought out.

Evaluation provides the thrust to refine goals and instructional objectives. It helps us see more clearly where we are going—in terms of both long-range and short-range goals. Without evaluation our perspective becomes clouded by circumstance and the feeling of the moment. Ministry—spiritually, musically, and educationally—demands accountability. Evaluation is that process.

REHEARSAL DISCIPLINE

If there is anything that seems to plague children's music directors it is discipline. Many fine directors are frustrated in their efforts to provide an excellent music ministry for children because of the discipline problem. Since music is a creative gift of God, an environment of strict military discipline is undesirable—most directors want it to be fun, and indeed it should be. But many, not wanting to make too many restrictions, are plagued by chaos, disorder, and confusion. The question seems to be, "Is there any way I can have a well-disciplined music rehearsal that is fun and will develop the creativity of the children?"

Four principles should be kept in mind. First, clearly understand that discipline is something you do for the child (or class) and not to him (or them). This means that discipline is the environment provided for a positive learning situation—not a punishment inflicted on an individual or the group. Discipline is from the old Latin word discipulae—"to learn." Learning thrives in a well-ordered environment. It has trouble surviving in chaos.

Second, we need to understand the difference between respect, rapport, and rules. A good learning environment— good discipline—is a combination of all three. Respect is earned. It is a reflection of the attitude the director demonstrates toward herself, the rehearsal content, and the children. Rapport is established. It is the continual building of relationships that results in mutual communication and in the child's feeling of individual significance. Rules are enforced. These are clearly established guidelines with clearly established consequences that are necessary for the successful operation of the class. When respect and rapport are properly in operation, rules can be kept to a minimum. Only when the teacher is incapable of earning respect or establishing rapport is an endless list of rules necessary.

Third, discipline requires consistency. Discipline and "teacher's pets" cannot co-exist. Discipline demands that the director treat all children fairly—all the time. And discipline demands that the director exhibit as much or more self-discipline than is expected from the children.

The fourth foundational principle for discipline is frequently called the "Law of Reinforcement," and was developed by two men—E. L. Thorndike and B. F. Skinner. Their law simply states, "Behavior which achieves desirable consequences will recur." The director needs to keep in mind that children like and *need* attention (so do grown-ups). A child would rather have negative attention than no attention at all. Many times we breed problems by never recognizing the children individually with praise and focused attention for their positive behavior. This kind of neglect is fertile ground for discipline problems. Some directors use various kinds of rewards—small prizes, points toward an award, or some other kind of tangible trinket. These may assist, but they should never take the place of the director's verbal praise. Research has found that verbal reinforcement can be the strongest motivation. Remember, we want to have our programs so fulfilling that the children love to learn for the fun of it and the personal reinforcement. An overemphasis on rewards gives the "I learned something for you, therefore you owe me something" attitude. Instead, we ought to foster the attitude, "I learned something for myself—something that I can enjoy. Learning is fun!"

Discipline requires preparation. Remembering that discipline is the environment we create for the child, and not retribution or punishment for misdeeds, it becomes obvious that it cannot be established on the spur of the moment. Children will always look for their limits because it is the limits that establish the security. Therefore we must plan and communicate the limits. It is wise for every director to know his options in advance. Establish these with your superior—church leader or school administrator. Once alternatives are known, a director should establish an order of consequences for use when the limits are violated. This preparation will make idle threats unnecessary, and nothing will defeat the credibility of a director more quickly than the use of idle threats. Communication with parents and leadership will clearly establish the fact that good discipline will be in operation at all times.

Expect the children to be good. Remember that behavior usually conforms to image. One of the reasons we find incorrigible students before the junior high level is that those children who have a reputation for being "troublemakers" are usually anticipated before arrival. It is unfair and unfortunate that teachers pass on tips regarding which children were the good ones and which were the bad ones. This reputation seems to pass from grade to grade with the child. Before long, the child knows he is a troublemaker. Everyone has told him so. Now all he has to do is live up to that reputation. It is amazing how a child responds when the director simply expects him to be a good student because he is a good kid. Avoid preconceived ideas. Expect the best and you just may astound everyone by getting it.

When you hit a behavior problem, isolate the cause as quickly as possible. Causes of poor discipline usually fit one of the four reasons—boredom, environment, insecurity, and least common, defiance. The most common cause of discipline problems is boredom. It is astounding to see how many teachers actually create their own discipline problems by boring the children. Boredom can result from lack of preparation or lack of momentum. Rehearsals that get bogged down with lots of verbal content from the director, or that run each activity to the point of monotony are prime candidates for boredom and misbehavior.

Children are also susceptible to environment. Inclement weather, dismal rooms, or sitting next to the wrong person can create havoc in a class. If the problem is caused by an environmental situation over which you have control, change it. Frequently a simple change in seating pattern will solve the problem. If the environmental cause is beyond your control—the weather, etc., help the children verbalize their feelings. This creates release for their frustration.

Some children misbehave because of insecurity. When you perceive this to be the problem, engage in a personal crusade to provide all the security possible for this youngster. Remember that children learn through experience. Lots of physical contact—appropriate for his age—lots of eye contact, and lots of focused attention will in time provide the security the child lacks. Don't expect changes overnight. But watch for gradual improvement and reinforce it in every way you can.

Of course there are those who create discipline problems because of direct defiance. Usually, however, this category is the smallest. When we run into a problem, to immediately assume that a child is being defiant is an unjustifiable conclusion. We must first assume that he is bored, there is an environmental problem, or he is insecure. Only after each of these causes has been ruled out are we safe to assume that a child is being defiant. Consequences of this misbehavior should be handled in accordance with your pre-established policy. Demerits, requiring parental attendance at rehearsal as a condition of participation, or removal from choir are appropriate consequences for defiant behavior.

Remember, when dealing with disciplinary situations, always address the individual by name. Anonymity fosters poor behavior. Name the offense. Communicate the consequences and above all, require a response. The response from the child creates the new understanding and agreement. It is always wise to ask a child, "Do you understand?" and expect a "Yes, Mr. _____," or "Yes, Mrs. _____." This not only communicates that the child understands, but the child recognizes that his agreement is with a certain person—the director. A muffled "um hum" will not have the same effect.

Finally, grant forgiveness. Children are like all other members of the human race. They make mistakes. Sometimes their behavior is a disappointment to themselves. That is not reason for isolation or endless prejudice. If there has been a problem, and it has been handled properly, as soon as possible give the child an opportunity to re-establish his worth—both in his own eyes, the eyes of his peers, and the eyes of the director. God's love is complete and unconditional. As his ministers, ours can be no less.

12
Perfecting Performances

Music comes alive through performance.
Ray Robinson

PERFORMANCE IS THE COMING TOGETHER of the music, the interpreter (conductor), the performers (the children), and the listeners (the audience). The added feature of the performers being children gives the sparkle of a "Christmas morning"—felt only when there are children involved. Anticipation, anxiety, and excitement permeate the atmosphere.

Performance, while not representative of the whole of a comprehensive children's music program, is a vital part. Most children love to perform. To deny them this opportunity after the consistent effort demanded by weekly rehearsals is demoralizing. Performance is a valuable learning experience. Children learn the rigors of prolonged discipline—required to put on an entire program. Children learn to stand before an audience—a valuable lesson in poise and self-confidence. Children learn self-control—standing still, focusing attention on the director, and putting aside individual needs for the overall effectiveness of the choir in responsible ministry. Children learn how to handle pressure in a productive way—using it to help them achieve beyond what they would without it.

If performance is too frequent—every week—the continual pressure blots out many vital aspects of a complete music education program. If, on the other hand, they perform too seldom—once or twice a year—there is significant drop in motivation and the development of performance skills. Performing two times a year simply does not provide enough consistency for the children to develop from one performance to another. Nor is it adequate to hold the interest of the majority for the extended intervals. This is one of the reasons so many children's choirs involve such a small percentage of the church children. Many times programs either discontinue rehearsals for a time in between performances or else have a tremendous influx of new children shortly before their program times. Either one of these characteristics is a symptom of an unhealthy children's music ministry.

The audience ought to be a consideration in planning a performance. Certainly a program within the church and a program given at a shopping center or civic club would have different personalities. Audiences respond better when not all the music has a foreign feel to it. Again, this doesn't mean that we will only perform the kind of music a church or school is used to—a tremendously confining perspective—but it does mean that we should vary our programs to generate response from the greatest number of people. Music that has all the same sound is of little educational benefit for the children and audience alike.

Performances need to be true representations of the program. The repertoire studied—whether psalms, hymns, or spiritual songs—needs to be the main substance of our performances. These programs can be amplified and personalized through the use of Scripture recitation (either individually or corporately), planned dialogue, characterizations in tableaux, or multi-media additions. Children are capable of performing a few well-learned songs approximately every six weeks. By the end of a quarter (three months) they are capable of contributing a major portion (approximately twenty-five minutes) of a church service. Musicals, while providing occasional variety and charm, are most effective if limited to one a year. Greater frequency simply distorts the other significant principles we have examined. Also, it is important that children learn to participate in services where they are not the "whole show," but a part of meaningful worship. Limiting their performances to complete musicals severely diminishes this perspective.

Children have a right to be excellent. Performances should not be inferior in quality because they are "just kids." Performances should be excellent precisely because they *are* children, and children are extremely capable. The attitude should not be one of tolerance but of significance, and significance is never born in mediocrity. If we set the standard of "only the best is good enough" we will get the best. If we set a lesser standard, we will achieve lesser results.

VOCAL PRODUCTION

Singing is a physical skill—requiring good breath support, good posture, an open throat, proper phonation and resonation, and good diction. We need to remember that children's voices are delicate instruments. To treat them carelessly can do more permanent damage than allowing an uncontrolled toddler to bang on an expensive grand piano.

Some people assume that "loud is good." These directors seem to confuse shouting with "singing out," and create a damaging hybrid. Shouting and singing out are not compatible. A child's playground voice and singing voice are not the same! Trying to combine them defies good melodic reproduction (the pitch is often poor and the intervals of the melody reproduced inaccurately) and good musical interpretation (phrasing and textual interpretation). Meaning is also lost—for both the performers and the audience. Children do not take time to think of the meaning of words when they are just shouting them out. They are more concerned with volume than verity!

Others rehearse their children with "tiny-tone, small-voice" concepts, causing the vocal production to be anemic, void of energy, vitality, and personality. Children are vivacious. They ought to sound vivacious when they sing. Thin tones are no more appropriate than harsh tones. Neither is desirable. The key to proper production is first to know what we are listening for, and then know how to achieve it.

A child's voice, when properly produced, should be clear and straight. It should not vibrate with the vibrato of an opera singer. It should never be strained, but should have a flute-like easy quality. It should be pleasant, never harsh. It should not come from the chest, but be generated by proper breathing and resonation. It should be clearly understood and not muffled or distorted—frequently referred to as "nasal" quality.

205

Children can participate in breathing exercises by placing their hands on their waist to feel the expansion of the diaphragm as air is inhaled and the contraction as air is exhaled. They can do breathing exercises by making a "train" formation—placing their hands on the waist of the person ahead of them and feeling the same physical phenomenon. Getting them to concentrate on breathing from the diaphragm avoids shallow upper-chest breathing that is characterized by the moving of the shoulders and upper-chest cavity.

Children can participate in vocal exercises with wide open vowels. Placing the hand at right angle to the body and resting the thumb on the breast bone with fingers pointing up to the mouth, and requiring the jaw to drop far enough to touch the fingers, helps the child drop his jaw, which reduces tension and produces an open sound. It also eliminates strain of the neck muscles—a sure sign of improper vocal production.

Children can experience focusing a tone (neither muffling nor distorting it) by placing their hand about twelve inches in front of their mouth and singing "to their hand." Invariably this brings the tone "out front" and brings clarity to the production and articulation.

Phonation—creating the desired kind of sound—can be done by having the children participate in a variety of sounds that take the source of air (breath support) and combine it with personality—such as sighing, whimpering, and exclaiming. Remember to conduct all vocal development exercises with good posture. The director should exhibit good posture—both standing and sitting and should require the same of the children. Since children cannot sit still for long periods of time, avoid extended vocal drills. Rather, intersperse them throughout the rehearsal.

Without articulation the beautiful sound has no meaning. How tragic to listen to any choir—children or adults—and not be able to understand their words. Poor diction is the result of laziness. Children need to work their tongue, lips, and jaw properly if the sound is to be understood. Frontal sounds are controlled by the tongue. Open sounds are controlled by the jaw. And combinations are controlled by the lips. The basic rule to remember is that the vowel carries the tone—sustain the pitch on your vowel sounds. Consonants make it understandable.

More in-depth examination and suggested vocalises are presented in the entries listed in the bibliography.

TECHNICAL PRODUCTION

Stage arrangements, miking, and lighting are technical aspects of performance that frequently suffer because of lack of knowledge and can diminish the effectiveness of the program. Many times this inferiority is excused because of budget limitations. Many possibilities, however, are available for the most economically minded director. Like any other task, it simply takes forethought.

In determining staging possibilities, begin by measuring the *usable* floor space. This figure will not include permanent fixtures—altar rail, non-movable podium, organ, piano, etc. Also, be sure to take into consideration the view of the audience. If the children are to be seen, take time to sit in various locations of the sanctuary and observe what are the visible areas of the stage. Avoid areas where visibility is obstructed.

Then, mark the location of the children. Will they be on risers? If so, be sure to measure correctly for their placement. The children should be able to stand comfortably—not squeezed, or you can expect problems. Will they all be standing together in the center of the platform, or will they be divided into two groups or even smaller ensembles? Remember to allow room for movement—especially if your program involves choreography or stage movement from place to place. Determine the location of soloists, lead characters, or narrators.

When this is done, you are ready to decide on possible additional staging effects. Sometimes you can design the staging first, especially if it is principally a backdrop or perimeter staging, as this will not substantially alter the available floor space, but may help determine the best placement for the children. Let the situation determine the sequence. Just be sure to address both areas.

Perimeter staging can be economically achieved by using "flats"—large pieces of muslin, stretched canvas, or particle board stretched over a frame of thin pieces of lumber and supported with braces from behind. If more than one scene is desired, you can connect three or four flats (one for each successive scene) into a triangle or cube and then simply rotate them at the appropriate time. This type of construction does not need supportive braces.

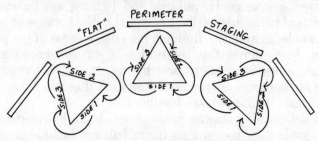

Open staging is also an economical, creative possibility. By open staging we mean the use of individual pieces to suggest an entire environment. A fence can suggest a yard, a table and chair can suggest a sitting room, a bed can suggest a bedroom, a log and a rock the countryside. It is not necessary to limit possibilities to closed staging. Many churches simply are not built to accommodate this kind of production. Open staging is portable and flexible.

In terms of stage movement, the most important principle is to *move on your own lines!* This means that one character should not be moving while another one is talking. Or the choir should not be moving during narration or individual spoken lines. Such movement divides the attention of the audience. Stage movement needs to help focus attention— not distract it. A character should take advantage of his own lines to move. A choir should engage in movement only when attention is to be focused on them—or time is allotted for movement when no one is the point of focus.

Platform or stage locations are always designated from the perspective of the person on stage facing the audience. "Down stage" is the front of the platform. "Up stage" is the rear. "Stage left" and "stage right" are from the view of the performer. Know and use the proper abbreviations:

Down stage .... DS
Up stage .... US
Stage right .... SR
Stage left .... SL

208

Then it becomes easy to notate locations and markings in your master score. In addition, you can assign movement ("blocking") by using three letters:

Down center stage .... DCS
Down stage right .... DSR
Down stage left .... DSL
Up stage right .... USR
Up center stage .... UCS
Up stage left .... USL

Diagrams can then be made for the conductor, lighting, and sound technicians for use in the dress rehearsals and performances. Simply mark the location of the speaker with an X, his movement with an arrow, and his final destination with another X.

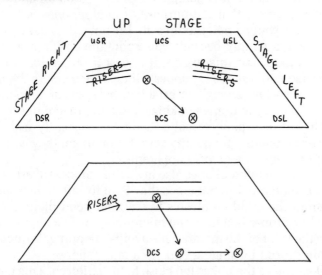

After you have determined your stage arrangement both for people and props, mark out the locations on the floor with masking tape. If children are standing on risers or in rows, have one of your volunteers place masking tape between the toes of the child—marking the location of his feet. Then with a black marking pen, print the name of each child on their specific piece of tape. This insures that they will end up in the same place for the performance that you put them in for the rehearsal. Solo positions or lead character placement can be marked with colored masking tape—use different colors for different characters.

Hopefully you will have walked through all stage movement many times in rehearsal. Keep it as nearly identical to what will happen in performance as possible. Mark the floor of the rehearsal the same way you will mark the platform floor. Then, when you walk through the performance in dress rehearsals, confusion will be at a minimum. If you are doing a musical that has several main characters, provide time for them to walk through their parts several times without the presence of the choir. This not only provides the security and focused attention they need to perform well, but it also prevents the chaos of having idle children around.

The use of microphones is another area involved in technical production. It is paramount that the director and children remember that *the purpose of microphones is to amplify the sound, not produce it.* Do not allow lazy vocal production simply because you know the children will be using mikes. For this reason, it is best if the children only rehearse with the microphones a time or two before the performance—just enough to establish balance for the sound technician, synchronize miking cues, and prevent the "stage fright" of new paraphernalia. If they consistently feel that the responsibility for quality sound is on *them*, they will not learn to rely on technical apparatus.

The use of microphones also makes the process of articulation even more difficult since they tend to garble the sound. Remind the children always to work for good diction. The level or proper height of the microphone is just slightly below the level of the mouth. This avoids "popping," and neck strain caused by singing "up" to a microphone.

Don't place the mikes too close to the children. This tends to pick up the voice of one or two children rather than the overall blend that you desire. Mikes that are on stands or booms (stands with an adjustable arm) are usually most suitable—ceiling mikes are usually designed for adult choirs and are too high for children's voices.

There are different kinds of microphones designed for different patterns of reception. The uni-directional mike receives sound stimulus from one direction. Its principle advantage is that it eliminates background and stray noises, and is not prone to feedback. Its disadvantage is that it can create "hot spots" since the sounds from closer voices are much louder than those further back.

Bi-directional microphones receive sound stimulus from two directions—180 degrees apart. They are usually not used for choral microphones, but may be useful if there are two groups or characters singing back and forth from positions opposite each other.

Omni-directional mikes pick up sound from all directions without discrimination. While they are suitable for singing in a circle, they are generally avoided in public address systems and choral performance because they create feedback.

Then there are different types of microphones. The condenser mike yields the most legitimate sound of any microphone. It is characterized by bright, crisp sound and excellent frequency for its small size. It does require a battery or power supply, however. One caution: Condenser microphones are very fragile. If they are dropped or knocked over they can be ruined or their performance greatly damaged. If you use condenser microphones, be sure you orient the children properly. They should not ever touch the equipment, and should always watch carefully when they are walking to avoid tripping or knocking over a mike stand.

The other type of microphone is the dynamic mike. It has good frequency, is very durable, and is usually less expensive. While condenser microphones should never be considered portable, dynamic microphones can stand up to the rigors of travel across the city or country. You will, however, sacrifice the quality of sound somewhat for this feature.

If the children use hand mikes for solos or individual speaking parts, they should keep a relaxed hand position and hold the microphone eight to twelve inches away from their mouth—and just below lip level. It is also a good idea to have a wind screen on the microphone to avoid "popping."

Speakers should always be above the audience level—never place them on the floor. Monitors should only be used when the children need to have reinforcement—either from instrumental trax or accompaniment that is "lost" in the auditorium. Children need to be able to hear themselves. Sometimes this is characteristic of the building and will be

211

accomplished without monitors. Other times they will open their mouths and feel the sound "die." This kind of acoustical problem needs to be dealt with by using monitors, as it is frightening for the children. They produce a sound, listen for it, hear nothing, and sing more softly so they can hear what it sounds like. Very shortly this cycle takes its toll—the children barely sing, and are barely heard.

If the children are standing on risers, have the microphones arranged at two heights—one for the bottom tier, and one midway between the top two tiers.

Number or codify each microphone with corresponding indications on the control board (mixer). Then it is easy to identify cues—such as "Turn microphone #3 on, turn off #5." Cue information will be of vital importance to the success of your program.

Lighting is accomplished by the use of two basic kinds of instruments—fresnels and ellipsoids. The fresnels (pronounced *fur-nel*) are basically used for area lighting because they dissipate the light, and have a "close throw"—which means they cannot throw the light for long distances. The ellipsoid, on the other hand, is capable of more direct focus and is available in varying lengths.

Additional effects can be achieved with the use of a follow spot or a strobe light, which creates a flashing effect. Color, both for skin tones and atmosphere creation, is accomplished through the use of gels—squares of colored material that fit into a frame at the front of the light. Warm colors produce a bright happy effect. Cool colors create a damp, dreary effect.

All lighting instruments should be connected to one central dimmer board (with the exception of the follow spot and strobe). These two function separately on their own power and should have separate operators. The lighting technician should operate only the dimmer board. All electrical connection should be done *only* by a competent electrician. Voltage of this nature should never be risked in the hands of an amateur.

Lighting instruments can be hung from a pole above the platform, or mounted on a lighting "tree" located at the center of the auditorium or in the rear corners. Since they are focused when they are mounted, it is essential that you have clearly marked the stage areas you intend to use.

Cue sheets are essential for all technicians. If you are embarking on a performance that has a lot of technical apparatus—orchestra, sound, lighting, and staging—you should consider enlisting a technical director to administrate and coordinate all these aspects. But regardless of whether or not you use a technical director, be sure that each technician has a complete script with blocking, miking, and lighting cues inserted. It is tragic when the children prepare diligently, and then their performance is hampered by technical incompetence. Most technical incompetence is the result of negligence. Many times a director simply did not communicate in advance what mikes were to be on at what point—and the children are not heard; or he didn't specify what lights were to be on at what time—and the children speak and move in darkness. Careful planning, communication (cue sheets) and practice will avoid these disappointments.

The basic guidelines for all technical aspects are: Keep them simple; keep them soft; keep them subtle. All technical paraphernalia is to enhance the ministry of the children—not overshadow it. If technical gimmickry distracts, it is inappropriate. If it enhances, it is suitable. It is the director's responsibility to be sure that these "benefits" of our technological age work to enhance and not destroy.

As the curtain opens on your children's performances, may the audience see a part of the meaning and potential of a comprehensive Christian music education for children. But may they sense in a much larger dimension that they are witnessing only a small part of your total ministry—a ministry that can give children the opportunity to actually become all that God has in mind for them to be—through worship, education, evangelism; cognitive, affective, and psychomotor learning; and enrichment of creative expression. This is children's music ministry.

BIBLIOGRAPHY
for Part Three

Alderson, Richard. *Complete Handbook of Voice Training.* West Nyack, New York: Parker Publishing Company, Inc., 1979.

Fortunato, Connie. *Music Is For Children.* Elgin, Illinois: David C. Cook Publishing Co., 1978.

Hilson, Stephen E. *What Do You Say to a Naked Spotlight?* Leawood, Kansas: Sound III, Inc., 1972.

Nye, Robert Evans, and Nye, Vernice Trousdale. *Music in the Elementary School.* Englewood Cliffs, New Jersey: Prentice-Hall, Inc., 1977.

Osbeck, Kenneth W. *The Ministry of Music.* Grand Rapids, Michigan: Kregel Publications, 1961.

Robinson, Ray, and Winold, Allen. *The Choral Experience.* New York: Harper's College Press, 1976.

INDEX